Molly

ALSO BY LOUISE GLÜCK

POETRY

Firstborn

The House on Marshland

Descending Figure

The Triumph of Achilles

Ararat

The Wild Iris

Meadowlands

Vita Nova

The Seven Ages

ESSAYS

Proofs and Theories: Essays on Poetry

AVERNO

AVERNO

LOUISE GLÜCK

FARRAR, STRAUS AND GIROUX

NEW YORK

Farrar, Straus and Giroux
18 West 18th Street, New York 10011

Distributed in Canada by Douglas & McIntyre Ltd.
Printed in the United States of America
Published in 2006 by Farrar, Straus and Giroux
First paperback edition, 2007

Grateful acknowledgment is made to the following publications, in whose pages these
poems first appeared: *The New Yorker*, *The New York Times*, *Poetry* ("Archaic Fragment,"
"Averno," and "The Evening Star"), *The Threepenny Review*, *Triquarterly*, and *Slate*.

"October" was originally printed in Sarabande Books as a chapbook in 2004.

"Omens" originally appeared in *After Pushkin* (Carcanet Press Ltd., 1999).

The Library of Congress has cataloged the hardcover edition as follows:
Glück, Louise, 1943–
    Averno / Louise Glück.—1st ed.
      p. cm.
    ISBN-13: 978-0-374-10742-0 (alk. paper)
    ISBN-10: 0-374-10742-4 (alk. paper)
    1. Persephone (Greek deity)—Poetry. I. Title.

  PS3557.L8A96 2006
  811'.54—dc22

                        2005042658

Paperback ISBN-13: 978-0-374-53074-7
Paperback ISBN-10: 0-374-53074-2

www.fsgbooks.com

10 9 8 7 6 5 4

for Noah

CONTENTS

AVERNO

Averno. Ancient name Avernus. A small crater lake, ten miles west of Naples, Italy; regarded by the ancient Romans as the entrance to the underworld.

THE NIGHT MIGRATIONS

This is the moment when you see again
the red berries of the mountain ash
and in the dark sky
the birds' night migrations.

It grieves me to think
the dead won't see them—
these things we depend on,
they disappear.

What will the soul do for solace then?
I tell myself maybe it won't need
these pleasures anymore;
maybe just not being is simply enough,
hard as that is to imagine.

I

OCTOBER

I.

Is it winter again, is it cold again,
didn't Frank just slip on the ice,
didn't he heal, weren't the spring seeds planted

didn't the night end,
didn't the melting ice
flood the narrow gutters

wasn't my body
rescued, wasn't it safe

didn't the scar form, invisible
above the injury

terror and cold,
didn't they just end, wasn't the back garden
harrowed and planted—

I remember how the earth felt, red and dense,
in stiff rows, weren't the seeds planted,
didn't vines climb the south wall

I can't hear your voice
for the wind's cries, whistling over the bare ground

I no longer care
what sound it makes

when was I silenced, when did it first seem
pointless to describe that sound

what it sounds like can't change what it is—

didn't the night end, wasn't the earth
safe when it was planted

didn't we plant the seeds,
weren't we necessary to the earth,

the vines, were they harvested?

2.

Summer after summer has ended,
balm after violence:
it does me no good
to be good to me now;
violence has changed me.

Daybreak. The low hills shine
ochre and fire, even the fields shine.
I know what I see; sun that could be
the August sun, returning
everything that was taken away—

You hear this voice? This is my mind's voice;
you can't touch my body now.
It has changed once, it has hardened,
don't ask it to respond again.

A day like a day in summer.
Exceptionally still. The long shadows of the maples
nearly mauve on the gravel paths.
And in the evening, warmth. Night like a night in summer.

It does me no good; violence has changed me.
My body has grown cold like the stripped fields;
now there is only my mind, cautious and wary,
with the sense it is being tested.

Once more, the sun rises as it rose in summer;
bounty, balm after violence.
Balm after the leaves have changed, after the fields
have been harvested and turned.

Tell me this is the future,
I won't believe you.
Tell me I'm living,
I won't believe you.

3.

Snow had fallen. I remember
music from an open window.

Come to me, said the world.
This is not to say
it spoke in exact sentences
but that I perceived beauty in this manner.

Sunrise. A film of moisture
on each living thing. Pools of cold light
formed in the gutters.

I stood
at the doorway,
ridiculous as it now seems.

What others found in art,
I found in nature. What others found
in human love, I found in nature.
Very simple. But there was no voice there.

Winter was over. In the thawed dirt,
bits of green were showing.

Come to me, said the world. I was standing
in my wool coat at a kind of bright portal—
I can finally say
long ago; it gives me considerable pleasure. Beauty

the healer, the teacher—

death cannot harm me
more than you have harmed me,
my beloved life.

4.

The light has changed;
middle C is tuned darker now.
And the songs of morning sound over-rehearsed.

This is the light of autumn, not the light of spring.
The light of autumn: *you will not be spared.*

The songs have changed; the unspeakable
has entered them.

This is the light of autumn, not the light that says
I am reborn.

Not the spring dawn: *I strained, I suffered, I was delivered.*
This is the present, an allegory of waste.

So much has changed. And still, you are fortunate:
the ideal burns in you like a fever.
Or not like a fever, like a second heart.

The songs have changed, but really they are still quite beautiful.
They have been concentrated in a smaller space, the space of the mind.
They are dark, now, with desolation and anguish.

And yet the notes recur. They hover oddly
in anticipation of silence.
The ear gets used to them.
The eye gets used to disappearances.

You will not be spared, nor will what you love be spared.

A wind has come and gone, taking apart the mind;
it has left in its wake a strange lucidity.

How privileged you are, to be still passionately
clinging to what you love;
the forfeit of hope has not destroyed you.

Maestoso, doloroso:

This is the light of autumn; it has turned on us.
Surely it is a privilege to approach the end
still believing in something.

5.

It is true there is not enough beauty in the world.
It is also true that I am not competent to restore it.
Neither is there candor, and here I may be of some use.

I am
at work, though I am silent.

The bland

misery of the world
bounds us on either side, an alley

lined with trees; we are

companions here, not speaking,
each with his own thoughts;

behind the trees, iron
gates of the private houses,
the shuttered rooms

somehow deserted, abandoned,

as though it were the artist's
duty to create
hope, but out of what? what?

the word itself
false, a device to refute
perception— At the intersection,

ornamental lights of the season.

I was young here. Riding
the subway with my small book
as though to defend myself against

this same world:

you are not alone,
the poem said,
in the dark tunnel.

6.

The brightness of the day becomes
the brightness of the night;
the fire becomes the mirror.

My friend the earth is bitter; I think
sunlight has failed her.
Bitter or weary, it is hard to say.

Between herself and the sun,
something has ended.
She wants, now, to be left alone;
I think we must give up
turning to her for affirmation.

Above the fields,
above the roofs of the village houses,
the brilliance that made all life possible
becomes the cold stars.

Lie still and watch:
they give nothing but ask nothing.

From within the earth's
bitter disgrace, coldness and barrenness

my friend the moon rises:
she is beautiful tonight, but when is she not beautiful?

In the first version, Persephone
is taken from her mother
and the goddess of the earth
punishes the earth—this is
consistent with what we know of human behavior,

that human beings take profound satisfaction
in doing harm, particularly
unconscious harm:

we may call this
negative creation.

Persephone's initial
sojourn in hell continues to be
pawed over by scholars who dispute
the sensations of the virgin:

did she cooperate in her rape,
or was she drugged, violated against her will,
as happens so often now to modern girls.

As is well known, the return of the beloved
does not correct
the loss of the beloved: Persephone

returns home
stained with red juice like
a character in Hawthorne—

I am not certain I will
keep this word: is earth
"home" to Persephone? Is she at home, conceivably,
in the bed of the god? Is she
at home nowhere? Is she
a born wanderer, in other words
an existential
replica of her own mother, less
hamstrung by ideas of causality?

You are allowed to like
no one, you know. The characters
are not people.
They are aspects of a dilemma or conflict.

Three parts: just as the soul is divided,
ego, superego, id. Likewise

the three levels of the known world,
a kind of diagram that separates
heaven from earth from hell.

You must ask yourself:
where is it snowing?

White of forgetfulness,
of desecration—

It is snowing on earth; the cold wind says

Persephone is having sex in hell.
Unlike the rest of us, she doesn't know
what winter is, only that
she is what causes it.

She is lying in the bed of Hades.
What is in her mind?
Is she afraid? Has something
blotted out the idea
of mind?

She does know the earth
is run by mothers, this much
is certain. She also knows
she is not what is called
a girl any longer. Regarding
incarceration, she believes

she has been a prisoner since she has been a daughter.

The terrible reunions in store for her
will take up the rest of her life.
When the passion for expiation
is chronic, fierce, you do not choose
the way you live. You do not live;
you are not allowed to die.

You drift between earth and death
which seem, finally,
strangely alike. Scholars tell us

that there is no point in knowing what you want
when the forces contending over you
could kill you.

White of forgetfulness,
white of safety—

They say
there is a rift in the human soul
which was not constructed to belong
entirely to life. Earth

asks us to deny this rift, a threat
disguised as suggestion—
as we have seen
in the tale of Persephone
which should be read

as an argument between the mother and the lover—
the daughter is just meat.

When death confronts her, she has never seen
the meadow without the daisies.
Suddenly she is no longer
singing her maidenly songs
about her mother's
beauty and fecundity. Where
the rift is, the break is.

Song of the earth,
song of the mythic vision of eternal life—

My soul
shattered with the strain
of trying to belong to earth—

What will you do,
when it is your turn in the field with the god?

1.
Who can say what the world is? The world
is in flux, therefore
unreadable, the winds shifting,
the great plates invisibly shifting and changing—

2.
Dirt. Fragments
of blistered rock. On which
the exposed heart constructs
a house, memory: the gardens
manageable, small in scale, the beds
damp at the sea's edge—

3.
As one takes in
an enemy, through these windows
one takes in
the world:

here is the kitchen, here the darkened study.

Meaning: I am master here.

4.
When you fall in love, my sister said,
it's like being struck by lightning.

She was speaking hopefully,
to draw the attention of the lightning.

I reminded her that she was repeating exactly
our mother's formula, which she and I

had discussed in childhood, because we both felt
that what we were looking at in the adults

were the effects not of lightning
but of the electric chair.

5.
Riddle:
Why was my mother happy?

Answer:
She married my father.

6.
"You girls," my mother said, "should marry
someone like your father."

That was one remark. Another was,
"There is no one like your father."

7.
From the pierced clouds, steady lines of silver.

Unlikely
yellow of the witch hazel, veins
of mercury that were the paths of the rivers—

Then the rain again, erasing
footprints in the damp earth.

An implied path, like
a map without a crossroads.

8.
The implication was, it was necessary to abandon
childhood. The word "marry" was a signal.
You could also treat it as aesthetic advice;
the voice of the child was tiresome,
it had no lower register.
The word was a code, mysterious, like the Rosetta stone.
It was also a roadsign, a warning.
You could take a few things with you like a dowry.
You could take the part of you that thought.
"Marry" meant you should keep that part quiet.

9.
A night in summer. Outside,
sounds of a summer storm. Then the sky clearing.
In the window, constellations of summer.

I'm in a bed. This man and I,
we are suspended in the strange calm
sex often induces. Most sex induces.
Longing, what is that? Desire, what is that?

In the window, constellations of summer.
Once, I could name them.

10.
Abstracted
shapes, patterns.
The light of the mind. The cold, exacting
fires of disinterestedness, curiously

blocked by earth, coherent, glittering
in air and water,

the elaborate
signs that said *now plant, now harvest*—

I could name them, I had names for them:
two different things.

11.
Fabulous things, stars.

When I was a child, I suffered from insomnia.
Summer nights, my parents permitted me to sit by the lake;
I took the dog for company.

Did I say "suffered"? That was my parents' way of explaining
tastes that seemed to them
inexplicable: better "suffered" than "preferred to live with the dog."

Darkness. Silence that annulled mortality.
The tethered boats rising and falling.
When the moon was full, I could sometimes read the girls' names
painted to the sides of the boats:
Ruth Ann, Sweet Izzy, Peggy My Darling—

They were going nowhere, those girls.
There was nothing to be learned from them.

I spread my jacket in the damp sand,
the dog curled up beside me.
My parents couldn't see the life in my head;
when I wrote it down, they fixed the spelling.

Sounds of the lake. The soothing, inhuman
sounds of water lapping the dock, the dog scuffling somewhere
in the weeds—

12.
The assignment was to fall in love.
The details were up to you.
The second part was
to include in the poem certain words,
words drawn from a specific text
on another subject altogether.

13.
Spring rain, then a night in summer.
A man's voice, then a woman's voice.

You grew up, you were struck by lightning.
When you opened your eyes, you were wired forever to your true love.

It only happened once. Then you were taken care of,
your story was finished.

It happened once. Being struck was like being vaccinated;
the rest of your life you were immune,
you were warm and dry.

Unless the shock wasn't deep enough.
Then you weren't vaccinated, you were addicted.

14.
The assignment was to fall in love.
The author was female.
The ego had to be called the soul.

The action took place in the body.
Stars represented everything else: dreams, the mind, etc.

The beloved was identified
with the self in a narcissistic projection.
The mind was a subplot. It went nattering on.

Time was experienced
less as narrative than ritual.
What was repeated had weight.

Certain endings were tragic, thus acceptable.
Everything else was failure.

15.
Deceit. Lies. Embellishments we call
hypotheses—

There were too many roads, too many versions.
There were too many roads, no one path—

And at the end?

16.
List the implications of "crossroads."

Answer: a story that will have a moral.

Give a counter-example:

17.
The self ended and the world began.
They were of equal size,
commensurate,
one mirrored the other.

18.
The riddle was: why couldn't we live in the mind.

The answer was: the barrier of the earth intervened.

19.
The room was quiet.
That is, the room was quiet, but the lovers were breathing.

In the same way, the night was dark.
It was dark, but the stars shone.

The man in bed was one of several men
to whom I gave my heart. The gift of the self,
that is without limit.
Without limit, though it recurs.

The room was quiet. It was an absolute,
like the black night.

20.
A night in summer. Sounds of a summer storm.
The great plates invisibly shifting and changing—

And in the dark room, the lovers sleeping in each other's arms.

We are, each of us, the one who wakens first,
who stirs first and sees, there in the first dawn,
the stranger.

There was a war between good and evil.
We decided to call the body good.

That made death evil.
It turned the soul
against death completely.

Like a foot soldier wanting
to serve a great warrior, the soul
wanted to side with the body.

It turned against the dark,
against the forms of death
it recognized.

Where does the voice come from
that says suppose the war
is evil, that says

suppose the body did this to us,
made us afraid of love—

ECHOES

1.

Once I could imagine my soul
I could imagine my death.
When I imagined my death
my soul died. This
I remember clearly.

My body persisted.
Not thrived, but persisted.
Why I do not know.

2.

When I was still very young
my parents moved to a small valley
surrounded by mountains
in what was called the lake country.
From our kitchen garden
you could see the mountains,
snow covered, even in summer.

I remember peace of a kind
I never knew again.

Somewhat later, I took it upon myself
to become an artist,
to give voice to these impressions.

3.

The rest I have told you already.
A few years of fluency, and then
the long silence, like the silence in the valley
before the mountains send back
your own voice changed to the voice of nature.

This silence is my companion now.
I ask: *of what did my soul die?*
and the silence answers

if your soul died, whose life
are you living and
when did you become that person?

FUGUE

1.

I was the man because I was taller.
My sister decided
when we should eat.
From time to time, she'd have a baby.

2.

Then my soul appeared.
Who are you, I said.
And my soul said,
I am your soul, the winsome stranger.

3.

Our dead sister
waited, undiscovered in my mother's head.
Our dead sister was neither
a man nor a woman. She was like a soul.

4.

My soul was taken in:
it attached itself to a man.
Not a real man, the man
I pretended to be, playing with my sister.

5.

It is coming back to me—lying on the couch
has refreshed my memory.
My memory is like a basement filled with old papers:
nothing ever changes.

6.
I had a dream: my mother fell out of a tree.
After she fell, the tree died:
it had outlived its function.
My mother was unharmed—her arrows disappeared, her wings
turned into arms. Fire creature: Sagittarius. She finds herself in—

a suburban garden. It is coming back to me.

7.
I put the book aside. What is a soul?
A flag flown
too high on the pole, if you know what I mean.

The body
cowers in the dreamlike underbrush.

8.
Well, we are here to do something about that.

(In a German accent.)

9.
I had a dream: we are at war.
My mother leaves her crossbow in the high grass.

(Sagittarius, the archer.)

My childhood, closed to me forever,
turned gold like an autumn garden,
mulched with a thick layer of salt marsh hay.

10.
A golden bow: a useful gift in wartime.

How heavy it was—no child could pick it up.

Except me: I could pick it up.

11.
Then I was wounded. The bow
was now a harp, its string cutting
deep into my palm. In the dream

it both makes the wound and seals the wound.

12.
My childhood: closed to me. Or is it
under the mulch—fertile.

But very dark. Very hidden.

13.
In the dark, my soul said
I am your soul.

No one can see me; only you—
only you can see me.

14.
And it said, you must trust me.

Meaning: if you move the harp,
you will bleed to death.

15.
Why can't I cry out?

I should be writing *my hand is bleeding*,
feeling pain and terror—what
I felt in the dream, as a casualty of war.

16.
It is coming back to me.

Pear tree. Apple tree.

I used to sit there
pulling arrows out of my heart.

17.
Then my soul appeared. It said
just as no one can see me, no one
can see the blood.

Also: no one can see the harp.

Then it said
I can save you. Meaning
this is a test.

18.
Who is "you"? As in

"Are you tired of invisible pain?"

19.
Like a small bird sealed off from daylight:

that was my childhood.

20.
I was the man because I was taller.

But I wasn't tall—
didn't I ever look in a mirror?

21.
Silence in the nursery,
the consulting garden. Then:

What does the harp suggest?

22.
I know what you want—
you want Orpheus, you want death.

Orpheus who said "Help me find Eurydice."

Then the music began, the lament of the soul
watching the body vanish.

II

THE EVENING STAR

Tonight, for the first time in many years,
there appeared to me again
a vision of the earth's splendor:

in the evening sky
the first star seemed
to increase in brilliance
as the earth darkened

until at last it could grow no darker.
And the light, which was the light of death,
seemed to restore to earth

its power to console. There were
no other stars. Only the one
whose name I knew

as in my other life I did her
injury: Venus,
star of the early evening,

to you I dedicate
my vision, since on this blank surface

you have cast enough light
to make my thought
visible again.

LANDSCAPE

The sun is setting behind the mountains,
the earth is cooling.
A stranger has tied his horse to a bare chestnut tree.
The horse is quiet—he turns his head suddenly,
hearing, in the distance, the sound of the sea.

I make my bed for the night here,
spreading my heaviest quilt over the damp earth.

The sound of the sea—
when the horse turns its head, I can hear it.

On a path through the bare chestnut trees,
a little dog trails its master.

The little dog—didn't he used to rush ahead,
straining the leash, as though to show his master
what he sees there, there in the future—

the future, the path, call it what you will.

Behind the trees, at sunset, it is as though a great fire
is burning between two mountains
so that the snow on the highest precipice
seems, for a moment, to be burning also.

Listen: at the path's end the man is calling out.
His voice has become very strange now,
the voice of a person calling to what he can't see.

Over and over he calls out among the dark chestnut trees.
Until the animal responds
faintly, from a great distance,
as though this thing we fear
were not terrible.

Twilight: the stranger has untied his horse.

The sound of the sea—
just memory now.

2.

Time passed, turning everything to ice.
Under the ice, the future stirred.
If you fell into it, you died.

It was a time
of waiting, of suspended action.

I lived in the present, which was
that part of the future you could see.
The past floated above my head,
like the sun and moon, visible but never reachable.

It was a time
governed by contradictions, as in
I felt nothing and
I was afraid.

Winter emptied the trees, filled them again with snow.
Because I couldn't feel, snow fell, the lake froze over.
Because I was afraid, I didn't move;
my breath was white, a description of silence.

Time passed, and some of it became this.
And some of it simply evaporated;
you could see it float above the white trees
forming particles of ice.

All your life, you wait for the propitious time.
Then the propitious time
reveals itself as action taken.

I watched the past move, a line of clouds moving
from left to right or right to left,
depending on the wind. Some days

there was no wind. The clouds seemed
to stay where they were,
like a painting of the sea, more still than real.

Some days the lake was a sheet of glass.
Under the glass, the future made
demure, inviting sounds:
you had to tense yourself so as not to listen.

Time passed; you got to see a piece of it.
The years it took with it were years of winter;
they would not be missed. Some days

there were no clouds, as though
the sources of the past had vanished. The world

was bleached, like a negative; the light passed
directly through it. Then
the image faded.

Above the world
there was only blue, blue everywhere.

3.

In late autumn a young girl set fire to a field
of wheat. The autumn

had been very dry; the field
went up like tinder.

Afterward there was nothing left.
You walk through it, you see nothing.

There's nothing to pick up, to smell.
The horses don't understand it—

Where is the field, they seem to say.
The way you and I would say
where is home.

No one knows how to answer them.
There is nothing left;
you have to hope, for the farmer's sake,
the insurance will pay.

It is like losing a year of your life.
To what would you lose a year of your life?

Afterward, you go back to the old place—
all that remains is char: blackness and emptiness.

You think: how could I live here?

But it was different then,
even last summer. The earth behaved

as though nothing could go wrong with it.

One match was all it took.
But at the right time—it had to be the right time.

The field parched, dry—
the deadness in place already
so to speak.

4.

I fell asleep in a river, I woke in a river,
of my mysterious
failure to die I can tell you
nothing, neither
who saved me nor for what cause—

There was immense silence.
No wind. No human sound.
The bitter century

was ended,
the glorious gone, the abiding gone,

the cold sun
persisting as a kind of curiosity, a memento,
time streaming behind it—

The sky seemed very clear,
as it is in winter,
the soil dry, uncultivated,

the official light calmly
moving through a slot in air

dignified, complacent,
dissolving hope,
subordinating images of the future to signs of the future's passing—

I think I must have fallen.
When I tried to stand, I had to force myself,
being unused to physical pain—

I had forgotten
how harsh these conditions are:

the earth not obsolete
but still, the river cold, shallow—

Of my sleep, I remember
nothing. When I cried out,
my voice soothed me unexpectedly.

In the silence of consciousness I asked myself:
why did I reject my life? And I answer
Die Erde überwältigt mich:
the earth defeats me.

I have tried to be accurate in this description
in case someone else should follow me. I can verify
that when the sun sets in winter it is
incomparably beautiful and the memory of it
lasts a long time. I think this means

there was no night.
The night was in my head.

5.

After the sun set
we rode quickly, in the hope of finding
shelter before darkness.

I could see the stars already,
first in the eastern sky:

we rode, therefore,
away from the light
and toward the sea, since
I had heard of a village there.

After some time, the snow began.
Not thickly at first, then
steadily until the earth
was covered with a white film.

The way we traveled showed
clearly when I turned my head—
for a short while it made
a dark trajectory across the earth—

Then the snow was thick, the path vanished.
The horse was tired and hungry;
he could no longer find
sure footing anywhere. I told myself:

I have been lost before, I have been cold before.
The night has come to me
exactly this way, as a premonition—

And I thought: if I am asked
to return here, I would like to come back
as a human being, and my horse

to remain himself. Otherwise
I would not know how to begin again.

A MYTH OF INNOCENCE

One summer she goes into the field as usual
stopping for a bit at the pool where she often
looks at herself, to see
if she detects any changes. She sees
the same person, the horrible mantle
of daughterliness still clinging to her.

The sun seems, in the water, very close.
That's my uncle spying again, she thinks—
everything in nature is in some way her relative.
I am never alone, she thinks,
turning the thought into a prayer.
Then death appears, like the answer to a prayer.

No one understands anymore
how beautiful he was. But Persephone remembers.
Also that he embraced her, right there,
with her uncle watching. She remembers
sunlight flashing on his bare arms.

This is the last moment she remembers clearly.
Then the dark god bore her away.

She also remembers, less clearly,
the chilling insight that from this moment
she couldn't live without him again.

The girl who disappears from the pool
will never return. A woman will return,
looking for the girl she was.

She stands by the pool saying, from time to time,
I was abducted, but it sounds
wrong to her, nothing like what she felt.
Then she says, *I was not abducted.*
Then she says, *I offered myself, I wanted
to escape my body.* Even, sometimes,
I willed this. But ignorance

cannot will knowledge. Ignorance
wills something imagined, which it believes exists.

All the different nouns—
she says them in rotation.
Death, husband, god, stranger.
Everything sounds so simple, so conventional.
I must have been, she thinks, a simple girl.

She can't remember herself as that person
but she keeps thinking the pool will remember
and explain to her the meaning of her prayer
so she can understand
whether it was answered or not.

I was trying to love matter.
I taped a sign over the mirror:
You cannot hate matter and love form.

It was a beautiful day, though cold.
This was, for me, an extravagantly emotional gesture.

. . . . your poem:
tried, but could not.

I taped a sign over the first sign:
Cry, weep, thrash yourself, rend your garments—

List of things to love:
dirt, food, shells, human hair.

. . . . said
tasteless excess. Then I

rent the signs.

AIAIAIAI cried
the naked mirror.

BLUE ROTUNDA

I am tired of having hands
she said
I want wings—

But what will you do without your hands
to be human?

I am tired of human
she said
I want to live on the sun—

.

Pointing to herself:

Not here.
There is not enough
warmth in this place.
Blue sky, blue ice

the blue rotunda
lifted over
the flat street—

And then, after a silence:

.

I want
my heart back
I want to feel everything again—

That's what
the sun meant: it meant
scorched—

    •

It is not finally
interesting to remember.
The damage

is not interesting.
No one who knew me then
is still alive.

My mother
was a beautiful woman—
they all said so.

    •

I have to imagine
everything
she said

I have to act
as though there is actually
a map to that place:

when you were a child—

    •

And then:

I'm here
because it wasn't true; I

distorted it—

    •

I want she said
a theory that explains
everything

in the mother's eye
the invisible
splinter of foil

the blue ice
locked in the iris—

.

Then:

I want it
to be my fault
she said
so I can fix it—

.

Blue sky, blue ice,
street like a frozen river

you're talking
about my life
she said

.

except
she said
you have to fix it

in the right order
not touching the father
until you solve the mother

      ·

a black space
showing
where the word ends

like a crossword saying
you should take a breath now

the black space meaning
when you were a child—

      ·

And then:

the ice
was there for your own protection

to teach you
not to feel—

the truth
she said

I thought it would be like
a target, you would see

the center—

      ·

Cold light filling the room.

I know where we are
she said
that's the window
when I was a child

That's my first home, she said
that square box—
go ahead and laugh.

Like the inside of my head:
you can see out
but you can't go out—

.

Just think
the sun was there, in that bare place

the winter sun
not close enough to reach
the children's hearts

the light saying
you can see out
but you can't go out

Here, it says,
here is where everything belongs

When Hades decided he loved this girl
he built for her a duplicate of earth,
everything the same, down to the meadow,
but with a bed added.

Everything the same, including sunlight,
because it would be hard on a young girl
to go so quickly from bright light to utter darkness.

Gradually, he thought, he'd introduce the night,
first as the shadows of fluttering leaves.
Then moon, then stars. Then no moon, no stars.
Let Persephone get used to it slowly.
In the end, he thought, she'd find it comforting.

A replica of earth
except there was love here.
Doesn't everyone want love?

He waited many years,
building a world, watching
Persephone in the meadow.
Persephone, a smeller, a taster.
If you have one appetite, he thought,
you have them all.

Doesn't everyone want to feel in the night
the beloved body, compass, polestar,
to hear the quiet breathing that says
I am alive, that means also
you are alive, because you hear me,
you are here with me. And when one turns,
the other turns—

That's what he felt, the lord of darkness,
looking at the world he had
constructed for Persephone. It never crossed his mind
that there'd be no more smelling here,
certainly no more eating.

Guilt? Terror? The fear of love?
These things he couldn't imagine;
no lover ever imagines them.

He dreams, he wonders what to call this place.
First he thinks: *The New Hell*. Then: *The Garden*.
In the end, he decides to name it
Persephone's Girlhood.

A soft light rising above the level meadow,
behind the bed. He takes her in his arms.
He wants to say *I love you, nothing can hurt you*

but he thinks
this is a lie, so he says in the end
you're dead, nothing can hurt you
which seems to him
a more promising beginning, more true.

I.

You die when your spirit dies.
Otherwise, you live.
You may not do a good job of it, but you go on—
something you have no choice about.

When I tell this to my children
they pay no attention.
The old people, they think—
this is what they always do:
talk about things no one can see
to cover up all the brain cells they're losing.
They wink at each other;
listen to the old one, talking about the spirit
because he can't remember anymore the word for chair.

It is terrible to be alone.
I don't mean to live alone—
to *be* alone, where no one hears you.

I remember the word for chair.
I want to say—I'm just not interested anymore.

I wake up thinking
you have to prepare.
Soon the spirit will give up—
all the chairs in the world won't help you.

I know what they say when I'm out of the room.
Should I be seeing someone, should I be taking
one of the new drugs for depression.
I can hear them, in whispers, planning how to divide the cost.

And I want to scream out
you're all of you living in a dream.

Bad enough, they think, to watch me falling apart.
Bad enough without this lecturing they get these days
as though I had any right to this new information.

Well, they have the same right.

They're living in a dream, and I'm preparing
to be a ghost. I want to shout out

the mist has cleared—
It's like some new life:
you have no stake in the outcome;
you know the outcome.

Think of it: sixty years sitting in chairs. And now the mortal spirit
seeking so openly, so fearlessly—

To raise the veil.
To see what you're saying goodbye to.

2.

I didn't go back for a long time.
When I saw the field again, autumn was finished.
Here, it finishes almost before it starts—
the old people don't even own summer clothing.

The field was covered with snow, immaculate.
There wasn't a sign of what happened here.
You didn't know whether the farmer
had replanted or not.
Maybe he gave up and moved away.

The police didn't catch the girl.
After awhile they said she moved to some other country,
one where they don't have fields.

A disaster like this
leaves no mark on the earth.
And people like that—they think it gives them
a fresh start.

I stood a long time, staring at nothing.
After a bit, I noticed how dark it was, how cold.

A long time—I have no idea how long.
Once the earth decides to have no memory
time seems in a way meaningless.

But not to my children. They're after me
to make a will; they're worried the government
will take everything.

They should come with me sometime
to look at this field under the cover of snow.
The whole thing is written out there.

Nothing: I have nothing to give them.

That's the first part.
The second is: I don't want to be burned.

3.

On one side, the soul wanders.
On the other, human beings living in fear.
In between, the pit of disappearance.

Some young girls ask me
if they'll be safe near Averno—
they're cold, they want to go south a little while.
And one says, like a joke, but not too far south—

I say, as safe as anywhere,
which makes them happy.
What it means is nothing is safe.

You get on a train, you disappear.
You write your name on the window, you disappear.

There are places like this everywhere,
places you enter as a young girl,
from which you never return.

Like the field, the one that burned.
Afterward, the girl was gone.
Maybe she didn't exist,
we have no proof either way.

All we know is:
the field burned.
But we *saw* that.

So we have to believe in the girl,
in what she did. Otherwise
it's just forces we don't understand
ruling the earth.

The girls are happy, thinking of their vacation.
Don't take a train, I say.

They write their names in mist on a train window.
I want to say, you're good girls,
trying to leave your names behind.

4.

We spent the whole day
sailing the archipelago,
the tiny islands that were
part of the peninsula

until they'd broken off
into the fragments you see now
floating in the northern sea water.

They seemed safe to me,
I think because no one can live there.

Later we sat in the kitchen
watching the evening start and then the snow.
First one, then the other.

We grew silent, hypnotized by the snow
as though a kind of turbulence
that had been hidden before
was becoming visible,

something within the night
exposed now—

In our silence, we were asking
those questions friends who trust each other
ask out of great fatigue,
each one hoping the other knows more

and when this isn't so, hoping
their shared impressions will amount to insight.

Is there any benefit in forcing upon oneself
the realization that one must die?
Is it possible to miss the opportunity of one's life?

Questions like that.

The snow heavy. The black night
transformed into busy white air.

Something we hadn't seen revealed.
Only the meaning wasn't revealed.

5.

After the first winter, the field began to grow again.
But there were no more orderly furrows.
The smell of the wheat persisted, a kind of random aroma
intermixed with various weeds, for which
no human use has been as yet devised.

It was puzzling—no one knew
where the farmer had gone.
Some people thought he died.
Someone said he had a daughter in New Zealand,
that he went there to raise
grandchildren instead of wheat.

Nature, it turns out, isn't like us;
it doesn't have a warehouse of memory.
The field doesn't become afraid of matches,
of young girls. It doesn't remember
furrows either. It gets killed off, it gets burned,
and a year later it's alive again
as though nothing unusual has occurred.

The farmer stares out the window.
Maybe in New Zealand, maybe somewhere else.
And he thinks: *my life is over.*
His life expressed itself in that field;
he doesn't believe anymore in making anything
out of earth. The earth, he thinks,
has overpowered me.

He remembers the day the field burned,
not, he thinks, by accident.
Something deep within him said: *I can live with this,
I can fight it after awhile.*

The terrible moment was the spring after his work was erased,
when he understood that the earth
didn't know how to mourn, that it would change instead.
And then go on existing without him.

OMENS

[handwritten: "union w/ the you didn't happen"]

I rode to meet you: dreams
like living beings swarmed around me
and the moon on my right side
followed me, burning.

[handwritten: "Very soul oriented"]

I rode back: everything changed.
My soul in love was sad *[handwritten: → heartbreak]*
and the moon on my left side
trailed me without hope.

To such endless impressions
we poets give ourselves absolutely,
making, in silence, omen of mere event,
until the world reflects the deepest needs of the soul.

after Alexander Pushkin

[handwritten notes:]
- Something abstract followed by something very realistic

- Complexity

- how could this relate to Persephone?
- Does it have an air of pessimism?
- why is it so vague in last line "thing"

Modern tone (handwritten, top)

TELESCOPE

There is a moment after (you) move your eye away
when you forget where you are   → fugue state
because you've been living, it seems,
somewhere else, in the silence of the night sky.
↳ somewhere peaceful/calm/ still

You've stopped being here in the world.
You're in a different place,
a place where human life has no meaning.

You're not a creature in a body.   ↳ beyond yourself (transcendental)
You exist as the stars exist,
participating in their stillness, their immensity.

→ Tommys point about the soul and the body
↓
body isnt what should or does matter

Then you're in the world again.
At night, on a cold hill,   } reality
taking the telescope apart.
↳ lonely tone

You realize afterward
not that the image is false   → still saw the stars
but the relation is false.   ↳ but you are not there w/ them

You see again how far away
each thing is from every other thing.   } how complex the universe is ↳ how complex we are

So vague (handwritten)

Left margin (handwritten, vertical): → relate to perception Poem → Doesnt find the answer

Bottom notes (handwritten):

- "you" → familiaranty/sense of imediacy
  ↳ 2nd person used 12 times
  ↳ picture urself in this position

- realistic poem → borders pessimism

- realizing complexity of Earth

▸ everyday life
  ↳ how we view things differently
  each so different
  ↳ creates DISCONNECT

71

Snow began falling, over the surface of the whole earth.
That can't be true. And yet it felt true,
falling more and more thickly over everything I could see.
The pines turned brittle with ice.

This is the place I told you about,
where I used to come at night to see the red-winged blackbirds,
what we call *thrush* here—
red flicker of the life that disappears—

But for me—I think the guilt I feel must mean
I haven't lived very well.

Someone like me doesn't escape. I think you sleep awhile,
then you descend into the terror of the next life
except

the soul is in some different form,
more or less conscious than it was before,
more or less covetous.

After many lives, maybe something changes.
I think in the end what you want
you'll be able to see—

Then you don't need anymore
to die and come back again.

PERSEPHONE THE WANDERER

1st. taken from her mother

In the second version, Persephone
is dead. She dies, her mother grieves—
problems of sexuality need not
trouble us here.

Compulsively, in grief, Demeter
circles the earth. We don't expect to know
what Persephone is doing.
She is dead, the dead are mysteries.

We have here
a mother and a cipher: this is
accurate to the experience
of the mother as

she looks into the infant's face. She thinks:
I remember when you didn't exist. The infant
is puzzled; later, the child's opinion is
she has always existed, just as

her mother has always existed
in her present form. Her mother
is like a figure at a bus stop,
an audience for the bus's arrival. Before that,
she was the bus, a temporary
home or convenience. Persephone, protected,
stares out the window of the chariot.

Lots of Questions

What does she see? A morning
in early spring, in April. Now

her whole life is beginning—unfortunately,
it's going to be
a short life. She's going to know, really,

73

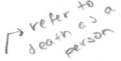
refer to a death as a person

only two adults: death and her mother.
But two is
twice what her mother has:
her mother has

one child, a daughter.
As a god, she could have had
a thousand children.

We begin to see here
the deep violence of the earth

whose hostility suggests
she has no wish
to continue as a source of life.

And why is this hypothesis
never discussed? Because
it is not *in* the story; it only
creates the story.

In grief, after the daughter dies,
the mother wanders the earth.
She is preparing her case;
like a politician
she remembers everything and admits
nothing.

For example, her daughter's
birth was unbearable, her beauty
was unbearable: she remembers this.
She remembers Persephone's
innocence, her tenderness—

What is she planning, seeking her daughter?
She is issuing
a warning whose implicit message is:
what are you doing outside my body?

You ask yourself:
why is the mother's body safe?

The answer is
this is the wrong question, since

the daughter's body
doesn't exist, except
as a branch of the mother's body
that needs to be
reattached at any cost.

When a god grieves it means
destroying others (as in war)
while at the same time petitioning
to reverse agreements (as in war also):

if Zeus will get her back,
winter will end.

Winter will end, spring will return.
The small pestering breezes
that I so loved, the idiot yellow flowers—

Spring will return, a dream
based on a falsehood:
that the dead return.

Persephone
was used to death. Now over and over
her mother hauls her out again—

[handwritten: u cant be @ peace in either places]

You must ask yourself:
are the flowers real? If

Persephone "returns" there will be
one of two reasons:

either she was not dead or
she is being used
to support a fiction—

I think I can remember
being dead. Many times, in winter,
I approached Zeus. Tell me, I would ask him,
how can I endure the earth?

And he would say,
in a short time you will be here again.
And in the time between

you will forget everything:
those fields of ice will be
the meadows of Elysium.

NOTES

"Landscape" is for Keith Monley.

"Archaic Fragment" is for Dana Levin.

"Thrush" is for Noah Max Horwitz and
Susan Kimmelman, in memory.

Irish Fairy
and
Folk Tales

FALL RIVER PRESS

New York

FALL RIVER PRESS

New York

An Imprint of Sterling Publishing
387 Park Avenue South
New York, NY 10016

Cover design: David Ter-Avanesyan

ISBN: 978-1-4351-5593-0

Manufactured in China

18 20 19 17

www.sterlingpublishing.com

Contents

Introduction

The fairy and folk tales collected in this volume are all reprinted from nineteenth-century sources, but they date back much farther, to a time when they were part of a centuries-old oral tradition and had yet to be committed to the printed page. These are stories that passed down through the ages, virtually unaltered in their telling. To the sophisticated, they were a record of long-held superstitions and quaint folk beliefs of the Irish peasantry. But to those who told and listened to them, they were not at all farfetched; rather, these stories expressed something fundamental about their culture and way of life. As William Butler Yeats wrote in the Introduction to his anthology *Fairy and Folk Tales of the Irish Peasantry* (1888), "They are the literature of a class for whom every incident in the old rut of birth, love, pain and death has cropped up unchanged for centuries: who have steeped everything in the heart: to whom everything is a symbol."

Collections of Irish fairy and folk tales played an important role in the Celtic Revival in literature and the arts, which was in full swing by the nineteenth century. Several of the writers represented in this book—notably T. Crofton Croker, William Carleton, and Lady Wilde (mother of Oscar)—made their reputations compiling them. Folklorists who recorded and collected such stories saw their work as a means of preserving storytelling traditions that were beginning to fade in the light of improved education and literacy. As "E.W.," author of the story collected here as "The Pooka" wistfully laments, "Now that 'the schoolmaster is abroad,' there can be no question that the warm sun of education will, in the course of a very few years, dissipate those vapours of superstition, whose wild and shadowy forms have from time immemorial thrown a mysterious mantle around our mountain summits, shed a darker horror through our deepest glens, traced some legendary tale on each unchiselled column of stone that rises on our bleakest hills, and peopled the green border of the wizard stream and sainted well with beings of a spiritual world."

The stories in this volume feature a wide variety of fantastic beings and creatures that appear in the folk tales of other cultures, among them ghosts, witches, changelings, and fairies (although the Irish have unique attitudes toward fairies—or, in folk terms, "the good people"—that distinguishes their relationship with them). Most, however, could only take place on Irish soil. In "A Legend of Knockmany," the mythic Celtic warrior hero, Cúchulainn (here named Cucullin), is reimagined as an invincible giant who meets his match in the crafty "Hibernian Hercules" Fin M'Coul. In Celtic folklore the pooka—an animal spirit that usually assumes the form of a rabbit, goat, or horse—can be good or bad; in the tale collected here as "The Pooka," the creature is unabashedly malevolent. "The Bunworth Banshee" features a being indigenous to Irish folklore: an elderly fairy woman whose wailing lament is a harbinger of impending death. Likewise, "The Lady of Gollerus" features a merrow, an amphibious creature of Gaelic legend who can be held captive in human form by anyone who takes possession of its *cohuleen druith,* or special diving cap. "The Lepracaun, or, Fairy Shoemaker" relates one of the best-known legends in Irish folklore: that elfin cobblers known as lepracauns (or, variously, leprechauns) possess crocks full of gold that are forfeit to any man who can catch one. Many different cultures have folk legends about deals with the devil, but Billy Dawson, the hapless hero of "The Three Wishes," outwits old Nick with ingenuity and irascibility that seem natural virtues of his Irish heritage.

Reflecting on the unique relationship that the Irish have with their folk heritage, William Butler Yeats wrote, "Even a newspaperman, if you entice him into a cemetery at midnight, will believe in phantoms, for everyone is a visionary if you scratch him deep enough. But the Celt is a visionary without scratching." The stories collected for *Irish Fairy and Folk Tales* are representative of the diversity of the Emerald Isle's colorful lore and legendry. They feature some of the finest examples of the fairy and folk tales that have become an inextricable part of the culture and character of the Irish people.

The Fairies

WILLIAM ALLINGHAM

Up the airy mountain,
    Down the rushy glen,
We daren't go a hunting
    For fear of little men;
Wee folk, good folk,
    Trooping all together;
Green jacket, red cap,
    And grey-cock's feather!

Down along the rocky shore
    Some make their home,
They live on crispy pancakes
    Of yellow tide-foam;
Some in the reeds
    Of the black mountain-lake,
With frogs for their watch-dogs,
    All night awake.

High on the hill-top
    The old King sits;
He is now so old and grey
    He's nigh lost his wits.
With a bridge of white mist
    Columbkill he crosses,
On his stately journeys
    From Slieveleague to Bosses;
Or going up with music
    On cold starry nights,
To sup with the Queen
    Of the gay Northern Lights.

They stole little Bridget
    For seven years long;
When she came down again
    Her friends were all gone.
They took her lightly back,
    Between the night and morrow,
They thought that she was fast asleep,
    But she was dead with sorrow.
They have kept her ever since
    Deep within the lakes,
On a bed of flagon-leaves,
    Watching till she wakes.

By the craggy hill-side,
    Through the mosses bare,
They have planted thorn-trees
    For pleasure here and there.
Is any man so daring
    To dig up one in spite,
He shall find the thornies set
    In his bed at night.

Up the airy mountain,
    Down the rushy glen,
We daren't go a hunting
    For fear of little men;
Wee folk, good folk,
    Trooping all together;
Green jacket, red cap,
    And grey-cock's feather!

The Priest's Supper

T. CROFTON CROKER

I t is said by those who ought to understand such things, that the good people, or the fairies, are some of the angels who were turned out of heaven, and who landed on their feet in this world, while the rest of their companions, who had more sin to sink them, went down further to a worse place. Be this as it may, there was a merry troop of the fairies, dancing and playing all manner of wild pranks on a bright moonlight evening towards the end of September. The scene of their merriment was not far distant from Inchegeela, in the west of the county Cork—a poor village, although it had a barrack for soldiers; but great mountains and barren rocks, like those round about it, are enough to strike poverty into any place: however, as the fairies can have every thing they want for wishing, poverty does not trouble them much, and all their care is to seek out unfrequented nooks and places where it is not likely any one will come to spoil their sport.

On a nice green sod by the river's side were the little fellows dancing in a ring as gaily as may be, with their red caps wagging about at every bound in the moonshine; and so light were these bounds, that the lobes of dew, although they trembled under their feet, were not disturbed by their capering. Thus did they carry on their gambols, spinning round and round, and twirling and bobbing, and diving and going through all manner of figures, until one of them chirped out—

"Cease, cease, with your drumming,
Here's an end to our mumming;
By my smell
I can tell
A priest this way is coming!"

And away every one of the fairies scampered off as hard as they could, concealing themselves under the green leaves of the lusmore, where if their little red caps should happen to peep out, they would only look like its crimson bells; and more hid themselves at the shady side of stones and brambles, and others under the bank of the river, and in holes and crannies of one kind or another.

The fairy speaker was not mistaken; for along the road, which was within view of the river, came Father Horrigan on his pony, thinking to himself that as it was so late he would make an end of his journey at the first cabin he came to, and according to this determination, he stopped at the dwelling of Dermod Leary, lifted the latch, and entered with "My blessing on all here."

I need not say that Father Horrigan was a welcome guest wherever he went, for no man was more pious or better beloved in the country. Now it was a great trouble to Dermod that he had nothing to offer his reverence for supper as a relish to the potatoes which "the old woman," for so Dermod called his wife, though she was not much past twenty, had down boiling in the pot over the fire; he thought of the net which he had set in the river, but as it had been there only a short time, the chances were against his finding a fish in it. "No matter," thought Dermod, "there can be no harm in stepping down to try, and may be as I want the fish for the priest's supper, that one will be there before me."

Down to the river side went Dermod, and he found in the net as fine a salmon as ever jumped in the bright waters of "the spreading Lee"; but as he was going to take it out, the net was pulled from him, he could not tell how or by whom, and away got the salmon, and went swimming along with the current as gaily as if nothing had happened.

Dermod looked sorrowfully at the wake which the fish had left upon the water, shining like a line of silver in the moonlight, and then, with an angry motion of his right hand, and a stamp of his foot, gave vent to his feelings by muttering, "May bitter bad luck attend you night and day for a blackguard schemer of a salmon, wherever you go! You ought to be ashamed of yourself, if there's any shame in you, to give me the slip after this fashion! And I'm clear in my own mind you'll come to no good, for some kind of evil thing or other helped you—did I not feel it pull the net against me as strong as the devil himself?"

"That's not true for you," said one of the little fairies, who had scampered off at the approach of the priest, coming up to Dermod Leary, with a whole throng of companions at his heels; "there was only a dozen and a half of us pulling against you."

Dermod gazed on the tiny speaker with wonder, who continued: "Make yourself no way uneasy about the priest's supper, for if you will go back and ask him one question from us, there will be as fine a supper as ever was put on a table spread out before him in less than no time."

"I'll have nothing at all to do with you," replied Dermod, in a tone of determination; and after a pause he added, "I'm much obliged to you for your offer, sir, but I know better than to sell myself to you or the like of you for a supper; and more than that, I know Father Horrigan has more regard for my soul than to wish me to pledge it for ever, out of regard to anything you could put before him—so there's an end of the matter."

The little speaker, with a pertinacity not to be repulsed by Dermod's manner, continued, "Will you ask the priest one civil question for us?"

Dermod considered for some time, and he was right in doing so, but he thought that no one could come to harm out of asking a civil question. "I see no objection to do that same, gentlemen," said Dermod; "but I will have nothing in life to do with your supper,—mind that."

"Then," said the little speaking fairy, whilst the rest came crowding after him from all parts, "go and ask Father Horrigan to tell us whether our souls will be saved at the last day, like the souls of good Christians; and if you wish us well, bring back word what he says without delay."

Away went Dermod to his cabin, where he found the potatoes thrown out on the table, and his good wife handing the biggest of them all, a beautiful laughing red apple, smoking like a hard ridden horse on a frosty night, over to Father Horrigan.

"Please your reverence," said Dermod, after some hesitation, "may I make bold to ask your honour one question?"

"What may that be?" said Father Horrigan.

"Why, then, begging your reverence's pardon for my freedom, it is, If the souls of the good people are to be saved at the last day?"

"Who bid you ask me that question, Leary?" said the priest, fixing his eyes upon him very sternly, which Dermod could not stand before at all.

"I'll tell no lies about the matter, and nothing in life but the truth," said Dermod. "It was the good people themselves who sent me to ask the question, and there they are in thousands down on the bank of the river waiting for me to go back with the answer."

"Go back by all means," said the priest, "and tell them, if they want to know, to come here to me themselves, and I'll answer that or any other question they are pleased to ask with the greatest pleasure in life."

Dermod accordingly returned to the fairies, who came swarming round about him to hear what the priest had said in reply; and Dermod spoke out among them like a bold man as he was: but when they heard that they must go to the priest, away they fled, some here and more there; and some this way and more that, whisking by poor Dermod so fast and in such numbers, that he was quite bewildered.

When he came to himself, which was not for a long time, back he went to his cabin and ate his dry potatoes along with Father Horrigan, who made quite light of the thing; but Dermod could not help thinking it a mighty hard case that his reverence, whose words had the power to banish the fairies at such a rate, should have no sort of relish to his supper, and that the fine salmon he had in the net should have been got away from him in such a manner.

The Changeling

LADY WILDE

A woman was one night lying awake while her husband slept, when the door suddenly opened and a tall dark man entered, of fierce aspect, followed by an old hag with a child in her arms—a little, misshapen, sickly-looking little thing. They both sat down by the fire to warm themselves, and after some time the man looked over at the cradle that stood beside the mother's bed with her boy in it, and kept his eyes on it for several minutes. Then he rose, and when the mother saw him walking over direct to the cradle, she fainted and knew no more.

When she came to herself she called to her husband, and bade him light a candle; this he did, on which the old hag in the corner rose up at once and blew it out. Then he lit it a second time, and it was blown out; and still a third time he lit the candle, when again it was blown out, and a great peal of laughter was heard in the darkness.

On this the man grew terribly angry, and taking up the tongs he made a blow at the hag; but she slipped away, and struck him on the arm with a stick she held in her hand. Then he grew more furious, and beat her on the head till she roared, when he pushed her outside and locked the door.

After this he lit the candle in peace; but when they looked at the cradle, lo! in place of their own beautiful boy, a hideous little creature, all covered with hair, lay grinning at them. Great was their grief and lamentation, and both the man and his wife wept and wailed aloud for the loss of their child, and the cry of their sorrow was bitter to hear.

Just then the door suddenly opened, and a young woman came in, with a scarlet handkerchief wound round her head.

"What are you crying for," she asked, "at this time of night, when every one should be asleep?"

"Look at this child in the cradle," answered the man, "and you will cease to wonder why we mourn and are sad at heart." And he told her all the story.

When the young woman went over to the cradle and looked at the child, she laughed, but said nothing.

"Your laughter is stranger than our tears," said the man. "Why do you laugh in the face of our sorrows?"

"Because," she said, "this is my child that was stolen from me to-night; for I am one of the fairy race, and my people, who live under the fort on the hill, thought your boy was a fine child, and so they changed the babies in the cradle; but, after all, I would rather have my own, ugly as he is, than any mortal child in the world. So now I'll tell you how to get back your own son, and I'll take away mine at once. Go to the old fort on the hill when the moon is full, and take with you three sheafs of corn and some fire, and burn them one after the other. And when the last sheaf is burning, an old man will come up through the smoke, and he will ask you what it is you desire. Then tell him you must have your child back, or you will burn down the fort, and leave no dwelling-place for his people on the hill. Now, the fairies cannot stand against the power of fire, and they will give you back your child at the mere threat of burning the fort. But mind, take good care of him after, and tie a nail from a horse-shoe round his neck, and then he will be safe."

With that the young woman took up the ugly little imp from the cradle in her arms, and was away before they could see how she got out of the house.

Next night, when the moon was full, the man went to the old fort with the three sheafs of corn and the fire, and burned them one after the other; and as the second was lighted there came up an old man and asked him what was his desire.

"I must have my child again that was stolen," he answered, "or I'll burn down every tree on the hill, and not leave you a stone of the fort where you can shelter any more with your fairy kindred."

Then the old man vanished, and there was a great silence, but no one appeared.

On this the father grew angry, and he called out in a loud voice, "I am lifting the third sheaf now, and I'll burn and destroy and make desolate your dwelling-place, if my child is not returned."

Then a great tumult and clamour was heard in the fort, and a voice said, "Let it be. The power of the fire is too strong for us. Bring forth the child."

And presently the old man appeared, carrying the child in his arms.

"Take him," he said. "By the spell of the fire, and the corn you have conquered. But take my advice, draw a circle of fire, with a hot coal this night, round the cradle when you go home, and the fairy power cannot touch him any more, by reason of the fire.

So the man did as he was desired, and by the spell of fire and of corn the child was saved from evil, and he grew and prospered. And the old fort stands to this day safe from harm, for the man would allow no hand to move a stone or harm a tree; and the fairies still dance there on the rath, when the moon is full, to the music of the fairy pipes, and no one hinders them.

The Lady of Gollerus

T. Crofton Croker

On the shore of Smerwick harbour, one fine summer's morning, just at day-break, stood Dick Fitzgerald "shoghing the dudeen," which may be translated, smoking his pipe. The sun was gradually rising behind the lofty Brandon, the dark sea was getting green in the light, and the mists clearing away out of the valleys went rolling and curling like the smoke from the corner of Dick's mouth.

"'Tis just the pattern of a pretty morning," said Dick, taking the pipe from between his lips, and looking towards the distant ocean, which lay as still and tranquil as a tomb of polished marble. "Well, to be sure," continued he, after a pause, "'tis mighty lonesome to be talking to one's self by way of company, and not to have another soul to answer one—nothing but the child of one's own voice, the echo! I know this, that if I had the luck, or may be the misfortune," said Dick, with a melancholy smile, "to have the woman, it would not be this way with me!—and what in the wide world is a man without a wife? He's no more surely than a bottle without a drop of drink in it, or dancing without music, or the left leg of a scissars, or a fishing-line without a hook, or any other matter that is no ways complete.— Is it not so?" said Dick Fitzgerald, casting his eyes towards a rock upon the strand, which, though it could not speak, stood up as firm and looked as bold as ever Kerry witness did.

But what was his astonishment at beholding, just at the foot of that rock, a beautiful young creature combing her hair, which was of a sea-green colour; and now the salt water shining on it, appeared, in the morning light, like melted butter upon cabbage.

Dick guessed at once that she was a Merrow, although he had never seen one before, for he spied the *cohuleen druith,* or little enchanted cap, which the sea people use for diving down into the ocean, lying upon the strand, near her; and he had heard, that if once he could possess himself of the cap, she would lose the power of going away into the water: so he seized it with all speed, and she, hearing the noise, turned her head about as natural as any Christian.

When the Merrow saw that her little diving-cap was gone, the salt tears—doubly salt, no doubt, from her—came trickling down her cheeks, and she began a low mournful cry with just the tender voice of a new-born infant. Dick, although he knew well enough what she was crying for, determined to keep the *cohuleen druith*, let her cry never so much, to see what luck would come out of it. Yet he could not help pitying her; and when the dumb thing looked up in his face, and her cheeks all moist with tears, 'twas enough to make any one feel, let alone Dick, who had ever and always, like most of his countrymen, a mighty tender heart of his own.

"Don't cry, my darling," said Dick Fitzgerald; but the Merrow, like any bold child, only cried the more for that.

Dick sat himself down by her side, and took hold of her hand, by way of comforting her. 'Twas in no particular an ugly hand, only there was a small web between the fingers, as there is in a duck's foot; but 'twas as thin and as white as the skin between egg and shell.

"What's your name, my darling?" says Dick, thinking to make her conversant with him; but he got no answer; and he was certain sure now, either that she could not speak, or did not understand him: he therefore squeezed her hand in his, as the only way he had of talking to her. It's the universal language; and there's not a woman in the world, be she fish or lady, that does not understand it.

The Merrow did not seem much displeased at this mode of conversation; and, making an end of her whining all at once—"Man," says she, looking up in Dick Fitzgerald's face, "Man, will you eat me?"

"By all the red petticoats and check aprons between Dingle and Tralee," cried Dick, jumping up in amazement, "I'd as soon eat myself, my jewel! Is it I eat you, my pet ?—Now, 'twas some ugly ill-looking thief of a fish put that notion into your own pretty head, with the nice green hair down upon it, that is so cleanly combed out this morning!"

"Man," said the Merrow, "what will you do with me, if you won't eat me?"

Dick's thoughts were running on a wife: he saw, at the first glimpse, that she was handsome; but since she spoke, and spoke too like any real woman, he was fairly in love with her. 'Twas the neat way she called him man, that settled the matter entirely.

"Fish," says Dick, trying to speak to her after her own short fashion; "fish," says he, "here's my word, fresh and fasting, for you this blessed morning, that I'll make you mistress Fitzgerald before all the world, and that's what I'll do."

"Never say the word twice," says she; "I'm ready and willing to be yours, mister Fitzgerald; but stop, if you please, 'till I twist up my hair."

It was some time before she had settled it entirely to her liking; for she guessed, I suppose, that she was going among strangers, where she would be looked at. When that was done, the Merrow put the comb in her pocket, and then bent down her head and whispered some words to the water that was close to the foot of the rock.

Dick saw the murmur of the words upon the top of the sea, going out towards the wide ocean, just like a breath of wind rippling along, and, says he, in the greatest wonder, "Is it speaking you are, my darling, to the salt water?"

"It's nothing else," says she, quite carelessly, "I'm just sending word home to my father, not to be waiting breakfast for me; just to keep him from being uneasy in his mind."

"And who's your father, my duck?" says Dick.

"What!" said the Merrow, "did you never hear of my father? he's the king of the waves, to be sure!"

"And yourself, then, is a real king's daughter?" said Dick, opening his two eyes to take a full and true survey of his wife that was to be.

"Oh, I'm nothing else but a made man with you, and a king your father;—to be sure he has all the money that's down in the bottom of the sea!"

"Money," repeated the Merrow, "what's money?"

"'Tis no bad thing to have when one wants it," replied Dick; "and may be now the fishes have the understanding to bring up whatever you bid them?"

"Oh! yes," said the Merrow, "they bring me what I want."

"To speak the truth then," said Dick, "'tis a straw bed I have at home before you, and that, I'm thinking, is no ways fitting for a king's daughter; so if 'twould not be displeasing to you, just to mention, a nice feather bed, with a pair of new blankets—

but what am I talking about? may be you have not such things as beds down under the water?"

"By all means," said she, "Mr. Fitzgerald— plenty of beds at your service. I've fourteen oyster beds of my own, not to mention one just planting for the rearing of young ones."

"You have," says Dick, scratching his head and looking a little puzzled. "'Tis a feather bed I was speaking of—but clearly, yours is the very cut of a decent plan, to have bed and supper so handy to each other, that a person when they'd have the one, need never ask for the other."

However, bed or no bed, money or no money, Dick Fitzgerald determined to marry the Merrow, and the Merrow had given her consent. Away they went, therefore, across the Strand, from Gollerus to Ballinrunnig, where Father Fitzgibbon happened to be that morning.

"There are two words to this bargain, Dick Fitzgerald," said his Reverence, looking mighty glum. "And is it a fishy woman you'd marry ?— the Lord preserve us!—Send the scaly creature home to her own people, that's my advice to you, wherever she came from."

Dick had the *cohuleen druith* in his hand, and was about to give it back to the Merrow, who looked covetously at it, but he thought for a moment, and then, says he—

"Please your Reverence, she's a king's daughter."

"If she was the daughter of fifty kings," said Father Fitzgibbon, " I tell you, you can't marry her, she being a fish."

"Please your Reverence," said Dick again, in an under tone, "she is as mild and as beautiful as the moon."

"If she was as mild and as beautiful as the sun, moon, and stars, all put together, I tell you, Dick Fitzgerald," said the Priest, stamping his right foot, "you can't marry her, she being a fish!"

"But she has all the gold that's down in the sea only for the asking, and I'm a made man if I marry her; and," said Dick, looking up slily, "I can make it worth any one's while to do the job."

"Oh! that alters the case entirely," replied the Priest; "why there's some reason now in what you say: why didn't you tell me this before?—marry her by all means if she was ten times a fish. Money, you know, is not to be refused in these bad times, and I may as well have the hansel of it as another, that may be would not take half the pains in counselling you that I have done."

So Father Fitzgibbon married Dick Fitzgerald to the Merrow, and like any loving couple, they returned to Gollerus well pleased with each other. Every thing prospered with Dick—he was at the sunny side of the world; the Merrow made the best of wives, and they lived together in the greatest contentment.

It was wonderful to see, considering where she had been brought up, how she would busy herself about the house, and how well she nursed the children; for, at the end of three years, there were as many young Fitzgeralds—two boys and a girl.

In short, Dick was a happy man, and so he might have continued to the end of his days, if he had only the sense to take proper care of what he had got; many another man, however, beside Dick, has not had wit enough to do that.

One day when Dick was obliged to go to Tralee, he left the wife, minding the children at home after him, and thinking she had plenty to do without disturbing his fishing tackle.

Dick was no sooner gone than Mrs. Fitzgerald set about cleaning up the house, and chancing to pull down a fishing net, what should she find behind it in a hole in the wall, but her own *cohuleen druith*.

She took it out and looked at it, and then she thought of her father the king, and her mother the queen, and her brothers and sisters, and she felt a longing to go back to them.

She sat down on a little stool and thought over the happy days she had spent under the sea; then she looked at her children, and thought on the love and affection of poor Dick, and how it would break his heart to lose her. "But," says she, "he won't lose me entirely, for I'll come back to him again, and who can blame me for going to see my father and my mother after being so long away from them?"

She got up and went towards the door, but came back again to look once more at the child that was sleeping in the cradle. She kissed it gently, and as she kissed it, a tear trembled for an instant in her eye and then fell on its rosy cheek. She wiped away the tear, and turning to the eldest little girl, told her to take good care of her brothers, and to be a good child herself, until she came back. The Merrow then went down to the strand.—The sea was lying calm and smooth, just heaving and glittering in the sun, and she thought she heard a faint sweet singing, inviting her to come down. All her old ideas and feelings came flooding over her mind, Dick and her children were at the instant forgotten, and placing the *cohuleen druith* on her head, she plunged in.

Dick came home in the evening, and missing his wife, he asked Kathelin, his little girl, what had become of her mother, but she could not tell him. He then inquired of the neighbours, and he learned that she was seen going towards the strand with a strange looking thing like a cocked hat in her hand. He returned to his cabin to search for the *cohuleen druith*. It was gone, and the truth now flashed upon him.

Year after year did Dick Fitzgerald wait expecting the return of his wife, but he never saw her more. Dick never married again, always thinking that the Merrow would sooner or later return to him, and nothing could ever persuade him but that her father the king kept her below by main force; "For," said Dick, "she surely would not of herself give up her husband and her children."

While she was with him, she was so good a wife in every respect, that to this day she is spoken of in the tradition of the country as the pattern for one, under the name of THE LADY OF GOLLERUS.

Pat Diver's Ordeal

Letitia Maclintock

Pat Diver, the tinker, was a man well accustomed to a wandering life, and to strange shelters: he had shared the beggar's blanket in smoky cabins; he had crouched beside the Still, in many a nook and corner, where poteen was made on the wild Innishowen mountains; he had even slept upon the bare heather, or in the ditch, with no roof over him but the vault of heaven; yet were all his nights of adventure tame and commonplace, when compared with one especial night.

During the day preceding that night, he had mended all the kettles and saucepans in Moville and Greencastle, and was on his way to Culdaff when night overtook him on a lonely mountain road.

He knocked at one door after another, asking for a night's lodging, while he jingled the halfpence in his waistcoat pocket, but was everywhere refused.

Where was the boasted hospitality of Innishowen, which he had never before known to fail?

It was of no use to be able to pay, when people seemed so churlish. Thus thinking he made his way towards a light a little further on, and knocked at another cabin door.

An old man and woman were seated one at each side of the fire.

"Will you be pleased to gie me a night's lodging, sir?" asked Pat, respectfully.

"Can you tell a story?" returned the old man.

"No, then, sir, I canna say I'm good at story telling," replied the puzzled tinker.

"Then you maun just gang further, for none but them that can tell a story will get in here."

This reply was made in so decided a tone, that Pat did not attempt to repeat his appeal, but turned away reluctantly to resume his weary journey.

"A story, indeed!" muttered he. "Auld wives' fables to please the weans!"

As he took up his bundle of tinkering implements, he observed a barn standing rather behind the dwelling house, and aided by the rising moon, he made his way towards it.

It was a clean, roomy barn, with a piled-up heap of straw in one corner. Here was a shelter not to be despised, so Pat crept under the straw and soon fell asleep.

He could not have slept very long when he was awakened by the tramp of feet, and peeping cautiously through a crevice in his straw covering, he saw four immensely tall men enter the barn, dragging a body, which they threw roughly upon the floor.

They next lighted a fire in the middle of the barn and fastened the corpse by the feet with a great rope, to a beam in the roof. One of them then began to turn it slowly before the fire. "Come on," said he, addressing a gigantic fellow, the tallest of the four, "I'm tired; you be to tak' your turn."

"Faix an' troth, I'll no turn him," replied the big man. "There's Pat Diver under the straw; why wouldn't he tak' his turn?"

With hideous clamour the four men called the wretched Pat, who, seeing there was no escape, thought it was his wisest plan to come forth as he was hidden.

"Now, Pat," said they, "you'll turn the corpse, but if you let him burn, you'll be tied up there, an' roasted in his place."

Pat's hair stood on end, and the cold perspiration poured from his forehead, but there was nothing for it but to perform his dreadful task.

Seeing him fairly embarked in it, the tall men went away.

Soon, however, the flame rose so high as to singe the rope, and the corpse fell with a great thud upon the fire, scattering the ashes and embers, and extracting a howl of anguish from the miserable cook, who rushed to the door, and ran for his life.

He ran on until he was ready to drop with fatigue, when seeing a drain overgrown with tall, rank grass, he thought he would creep in there, and lie hidden till morning.

But he had not been many minutes in the drain before he heard the heavy trampling again, and the four men came up with their burden, which they laid down on the edge of the drain.

"I'm tired," said one, to the giant, "it's your turn to carry him a piece now."

"Faix an' troth I'll no carry him," replied he, "but there's Pat Diver in the drain; why wouldn't he come out an' tak' his turn?"

"Come out, Pat! come out!" roared all the men, and Pat, almost dead with fright, crept out.

He staggered on under the weight of the corpse until he reached Kiltown Abbey, at ruin festooned with ivy, where the brown owl hooted all night long, and the forgotten dead slept around the walls, under dense, matted tangles of brambles and benweed.

No one ever buried there now, but Pat's tall companions turned into the wild graveyard, and began to dig a grave.

Pat seeing them thus engaged, thought he might once more try to escape, and climbed up into a hawthorn tree in the fence, hoping to be hidden by the boughs.

"I'm tired," said the man who was digging the grave, "here, tak' the spade," addressing the big man, "it's your turn."

"Faix an' troth, it's no my turn," replied he, as before. "There's Pat Diver in the tree: why wouldn't he come down an' tak' his turn?"

Pat came down to take the spade, but just then the cocks in the little farmyards and cabins round the Abbey began to crow, and the men looked at one another.

"We must go," said they, "an' well it is for you, Pat Diver, that the cocks crowed, for if they had not, you'd just ha' been bundled into thon grave wi' the corpse."

Two months passed, and Pat had wandered far and wide over the county Donegal, when he chanced to arrive at Raphoe during a fair.

Among the crowd that filled the Diamond he came suddenly upon the big man.

"How are you, Pat Diver?" said he, bending down to look in the tinker's face.

"You've the advantage of me, sir, for I havena' the pleasure of knowing you," faltered Pat.

"Do you not know me, Pat? Whisper—when you go back to Innishowen, you'll have a story to tell!"

The Pooka

E. W.

Goblins haunt from fire or fen.
Or mine, or flood, to the walks of men.
—*Collins*

Now that "the schoolmaster is abroad," there can be no question that the warm sun of education will, in the course of a very few years, dissipate those vapours of superstition, whose wild and shadowy forms have from time immemorial thrown a mysterious mantle around our mountain summits, shed a darker horror through our deepest glens, traced some legendary tale on each unchiselled column of stone that rises on our bleakest hills, and peopled the green border of the wizard stream and sainted well with beings of a spiritual world. While, however, the friends of Ireland cannot but be pleased in thinking that our peasantry should, from being better informed, renounce their belief in these idle tales of superstition, to which they, unfortunately, have for centuries been taught to listen with delight, to the exclusion of matters more rational and more important; it is to be hoped that the two prominent features of our antiquity as a nation, will not be altogether lost sight of—namely, our vernacular language, and those extraordinary legends, which are esteemed by many as going a great length to prove—from their remarkable analogy with the tales of the eastern world—our oriental descent. Although "the good people" still retain a most respectable footing, a peasant may now travel from Cape Clear to Cunnemara without encountering that once dreaded personage, a ghost. Even the *Pooka,* or Irish goblin, has not for the last forty years, as far as our recollection serves, been known to shake the dripping ooze from his hairy hide, to approach the haunts of men, or to practise by the conscious light of the moon, like the fairies and satyrs of heathen mythology, any of those unlucky tricks upon his mortal neighbours, for which be was at one period so much dreaded in many portions of our island.

The Pooka is described as a frisky mischievous being, having such a turn for roguish fun, as to induce him to be all night in wait for the *carough* returning over the moor from the pleasures of the card-table, or for the frequenter of wakes. His usual appearance was that of a sturdy pony, with a shaggy hide. He generally lay couched like a cat in the pathway of the unfortunate pedestrian, then starting between his legs, he hoisted the unlucky wretch aloft on his crupper, from which no shin-breaking rushings by stone walls, no furious driving through white-thorn hedges, or life-shaking plunges down cliff and quagmire, could unseat him. The first crowing of the March cock respited the sorrow-ful rider, who generally ended this dear-bought tour by a tremendous fling from the pooka's back into some deep bog-hole, or thorny-brake, where ten thousand prickles reared their points to drink the blood of his bruised and broken flesh. On the other hand, he is reported to commisserate the lot of the benighted traveller; and there are some instances on record of his having gently trotted beneath the way-faring cottager for many a mile to the neighbourhood of the well-remembered cabin on the heath.

Feah-a-Pooka, in the county of Kerry, was, as its name imports, the haunt of one of those imaginary monsters. This feah, or marsh, belonged to Tim Dorney, a snug farmer, whose ancestors for many years occupied the adjacent farm, and who, honest men, in that golden age, never found it necessary to disturb the goblin in the favourite haunt, by reclaiming his dreary abode. But when the farm which his grandfather tilled came into Tim Dorney's occupation, a taste for improvement, and the necessary expenditure of a large and increasing family, induced him to cross-cut Feah-a-Pooka by drains and ditches; and two summers had hardly passed, when this haunt of the wild goose and the dark mischievous goblin, afforded a heavy sward of hay, and firm footing for man and beast. The pooka, thus beaten up and driven from the marsh, naturally turned his thoughts to the meditation of revenge on him who, with profane hand, rent asunder that sacred veil which the superstition of ages had woven round the dreaded spot.

Tim was a painstaking, industrious peasant, and accustomed to traverse his farm every night, to ascertain that no neighbouring cattle trespassed on his ground. One night, as he returned along the border of the marsh, he saw something shaped like a dark-coloured, long-tailed pony lie in the narrow way, directly across his path; and before he could slip aside, to shun the lurking apparition, the pooka (for it was he) suddenly started between the legs of the terrified farmer, and bore him off the ground. The goblin rushed along with the speed of the whirlwind, and Tim's first moment of reflection was employed in a fruitless attempt to fling himself to the ground; but he found that some invisible hand had bound him to the back of his supernatural enemy. It would be tedious to recount the hard rubbings against stone walls, and the wild rushings through quickset hedges, that Tim Dorney endured, while the rapidity of his flight completely deprived him of breath and utterance. At last they rushed towards a tall cliff, which frowned in horrid gloom above the deep river, and intercepted, by its giant bulk, the yellow light of the moon that gilt the mountain tops, quivered in the rustling foliage of the trees, and, brightening in its advance, burnished the trembling waters with liquid fire. The pooka pushed with unabated speed to the edge of the rock—then suddenly stopped, as if to add to the death-pang of his agonised victim, by a previous view of the fearful height and the dark waves that curled among the pointed rocks below. Tim Dorney now concluding that all of his life would be ended for him in the next plunge, yelled a shriek of unutterable dismay. The tall cliff returned the piercing sound, which with the scream of the startled wildfowl, and the demon voice of the pooka, that combined the mockery of human laughter with a wild, indescribable howl, blended in horrid unison along the lonely glen. Whether the pooka was satisfied with thus inflicting the pangs of a frightful death by anticipation, or that he possessed no power over human life, does not appear; but in the next moment he started from the fearful cliff, and returning through the deep ravines and tangled underwood, to a furze brake that skirted the border of a standing pool, plunged his unfortunate rider among the sharp bushes. Happy in his deliverance, he heard the troubled waters of the dark pool resound to the plunge of the returning pooka—beheld his uncouth figure glance darkly along the moor, till the lessening form grew dimly

faint in the moonshine—and the hurried splash-
ing of his rapid hoof broke the silence of the night
no more. Tim, as may naturally be supposed, made
the best of his way to the cottage; and being of true
Milesian origin, determined on having his revenge
upon his fiendish enemy.

It was a fine night in the month of August,
when Tim Dorney, having sufficiently recruited
himself after his adventure of wild horsemanship,
walked forth, like him "that hath his quarrel just,"
doubly armed. His heels were furnished with a pair
of long-necked spurs, that bore rowels contrived
at the next forge, which could goad a rhinoceros
to death. His hand wielded a loaden whip, so
called from the handle being set with lead, and in
the grasp of a strong man was capable of felling
an ox. "He whistled as he went," not "for want of
thought," for his mind was brooding over a plan
of revenge against the pooka, who, according to
his usual habit, started between the farmer's legs,
and bore him off! Tim, nothing loth at the abduc-
tion, just when the pooka was commencing his
antics, twisted the lash of the whip round his hand,
and levelled such blows about the goblin's ears,
as would have crushed any skull made of mortal,
penetrable stuff, while the sharp-roweled spurs
gave ample revenge for the pointed insults of the
preceding night. "Dire were the tossings, deep
the groans," of the pooka during this unmerciful
ride; but Tim Dorney clung to him like a monkey,

until the pooka lay down, outmastered by his mortal antagonist. Next night, Tim walked abroad in quest of his acquaintance. He whistled his favourite air of "Tham-a-hulla," to lull the suspicions of the latter, who held aloof, quite on his guard, eying the other from his lurking-place, and breaking his usual taciturnity by asking, in an uncouth voice, the well-remembered question, "*A will na gerane urth?*" ("Have you sharp things on?")

Some years had now rolled their seasons round, and the pooka seemed to have entirely forgotten his antagonist, and his ancient dwelling of the marsh, when Tim Dorney had occasion to visit a gossip's sister's cousin's brother-in-law, who had lately come home after an absence of twenty-five years on board a man of war. The credit side of the account-sheet of this seaman's life was fraught with a copious list of wonders—"all his travels' history"—and a pension of nine-pence a day. On the debtor side stood the loss of the right arm, the closing of his starboard eye, and sundry minor details, received in the duty of boarding and cutting out, with occasional tavern scuffles. Tim was highly delighted at the "tough yarn" of his old acquaintance—heard with "gaping wonderment" the recital of a battle with a French seventy-four off the island of *Elbow* (Elba), where the relater lost his precious *arm;* an encounter with a Salee rover, which they sent down to *Old Davy;* and a dreadful storm near the island of *Moll Tow* (Malta); of voyages along the coast of *Tunis,* where the people are all *musicianers*; by *Tripoli,* famous for its *wrestlers*; and a journey through the desert of *Barka,* where the inhabitants, men and women, have *dog's heads!* The ale of a neighbouring *shebeen* greatly improved the sailor's turn for narration; and though the rain poured in torrents through the grass-grown roof of the cabin, yet

> "The night flew on with songs an' clatter,
> And aye the ale was growing better."

But Tim being retained that night to form one of a party that had engaged to play at cards for two hundred of herrings, and as he was a famous *carough,* he could not disappoint his friends, who mainly depended on Tim's address to carry off the wager. The rain had now ceased, and after grasping the sailor's hand, and requesting his company on a given night at Feah-a-Pooka, he departed. The moon, yet obscured by heavy clouds, cast a sad and sickly gleam along his path, which winding round a precipitous descent, led into the bosom of a deep glen, where the turbid mountain torrents had swelled into muddy waves the clear and beautiful brook, that erewhile had bubbled with soothing murmurs along the yellow pebbles. There was no sound on the hill, save the plaintive howl of the watch-dog, baying the broad round moon. The night wind slightly shook the thin foliage of the decaying wood that surmounted the steep sides of the glen, and the hoarse, hollow sound of the roaring river, that would seem to a fanciful ear the boding voice of the water fairy, echoed along the distant banks. Though Tim Dorney's education had taught him to people the loneliest scenes with beings of another life, yet he passed unappalled to the brink of the torrent, and sighed to behold that the force of the stream left him little chance of crossing over with safety. While he loitered along the bank, he was agreeably surprised to behold in a little cove, which led into a ford, a small horse, resembling a Kerry pony. He was tied by a halter, had a *pilleen susa*, or straw saddle, on his back, and into one of the foldings of the straw saddle was stuck a *whitethorn* plant. Tim, grateful for this favourable opportunity of moving homeward, had already his leg raised to mount, when the titter of suppressed laughter behind a crag, shook his heart with terror, and excited his suspicion of the pony. He had not meddled with the whitethorn stick, for he rarely went abroad by day or night unprovided with a choice hazel sapling. This miraculous plant, against which nothing evil can contend, well served this time of need; for retiring a little, Tim Dorney bestowed so hearty a salute on the guileful pooka, (for it was he,) that the laughter sounds were changed into a wild howl, and as the pooka disappeared along the troubled stream, the dashing waters deluged the sounding banks.

But a time arrived when the persevering goblin wreaked cruel revenge on his hitherto fortunate adversary. It was approaching the 25th of March, when the farmers usually pay the rent; and Tim, who was extremely punctual in the payment of the half-year's gale, prepared to send a quantity of the last season's butter to Cork for that purpose. Wheel carriages were then totally unknown in that part of the country—"the sliding car, indebted to no wheels," glided in the vicinity of the farms, while burdens were conveyed to more remote places on the backs of horses. Five or six neighbours at this time were setting off to transmit the produce of the dairy to Cork, and Tim, with four stunted nags that usually ran wild and free on the mountains, fell into their company. Each little horse was generally laden with two *fullbounds* of butter; but one or two, whose owners were unable to furnish the even number of firkins, carried a large stone placed on the opposite side to balance the single one. After journeying all night, on the next morning an accident happened to Tim Dorney in his way through Millstreet, that seemed the type and forerunner of the evening's misfortune. As the *Kerry dragoons* marched in long procession through the single street that composes this little town, the drummer of a company of soldiers stationed in the barrack, "beat the doubling drum," with such "furious heat" as set all the ponies prancing beneath their riders and butter-firkins. It happened that the nag on which Tim rode, by an unfortunate curvette on the slippery pavement, had his heels tripped up, and he fell under the load that lumbered on his back. The rider, whose Milesian irascibility was not much allayed at having the accident perpetrated by a *red coat,* drew his trusty *hazel* from its resting place between the firkins, and by its instantaneous application to the drummer's head forced him to bite the dust. Though the drummer, for certain s*triking* reasons, was no favourite with his comrades, yet a sentinel, who witnessed this insult to the *cloth,* levelled Tim with the butt end of his piece. The alarm being given, the soldiers rushed thick and fast to assault the *Kerry dragoons,* and as quick rushed the town-folk to their support. The reader's imagination must supply what I would fail in delineating: it will suffice to tell, that after some broken heads and bayonet thrusts on both sides, the red-coats retreated to their strong-hold, and the triumphant Kerryonians were escorted by their faithful allies to the summit of Mushra mountain.

In the evening, the caravan came within view of Blarney Castle, while the last rays of the declining sun tinged its ivied turrets with golden hue. As the night breeze blew keen and fierce, our travellers halted at a small public-house on the road, to repel its chilling influence by a glass of spirits. Their delay was hardly for a minute, and they hastened to overtake the horses that moved at a slow pace before them; but suddenly some strange disorder began to prevail among the animals: some fled terrified along the road—others ran across the open

common that extended to the right—and Tim
Dornev's train, particularly, were observed to reach
a fearful and perpendicular descent, from whose
edge the road lay about twenty yards. Their terri-
fied owner uttered a shriek of dread and despair,
when he beheld the misshapen, hairy pooka urge
his cattle to the steep cliff. It was only the work
of a moment—they rushed as if by an irresistible
impulse to the fatal brink, and, tumbling head-
long, one instant beheld their shattered, lifeless
carcasses strew the bottom of the stream-worn
ravine; the pointed rocks below staved the butter-
casks to pieces, and their contents were wholly
lost. This was but the commencement of a train of
misfortune to Tim Dorney. He was finally ejected
from his snug, well-improved farm. Feah-a-Pooka,
that had been in the occupation of his family for
a hundred and fifty years before, passed into the
hands of strangers; and the descendants of Tim
Dorney are homeless wanderers on the earth; and
such is the account which at this day is given by
the remaining members of the family, of the com-
mencement of their misfortunes.

The Bunworth Banshee

T. CROFTON CROKER

The Reverend Charles Bunworth was rector of Buttevant, in the county of Cork, about the middle of the last century. He was a man of unaffected piety, and of sound learning; pure in heart, and benevolent in intention. By the rich he was respected, and by the poor beloved; nor did a difference of creed prevent their looking up to "*the minister*" (so was Mr. Bunworth called by them) in matters of difficulty and in seasons of distress, confident of receiving from him the advice and assistance that a father would afford to his children. He was the friend and the benefactor of the surrounding country—to him, from the neighbouring town of Newmarket, came both Curran and Yelverton for advice and instruction, previous to their entrance at Dublin College. Young, indigent, and inexperienced, these afterwards eminent men received from him, in addition to the advice they sought, pecuniary aid;

and the brilliant career which was theirs, justified the discrimination of the giver.

But what extended the fame of Mr. Bunworth, far beyond the limits of the parishes adjacent to his own, was his performance on the Irish harp, and his hospitable reception and entertainment of the poor harpers who travelled from house to house about the country. Grateful to their patron, these itinerant minstrels sang his praises to the tingling accompaniment of their harps, invoking in return for his bounty abundant blessings on his white head, and celebrating in their rude verses the blooming charms of his daughters, Elizabeth and Mary. It was all these poor fellows could do; but who can doubt that their gratitude was sincere, when, at the time of Mr. Bunworth's death, no less than fifteen harps were deposited on the loft of his granary, bequeathed to him by the last members of a race which has now ceased to exist. Trifling, no doubt, in intrinsic value were these relics, yet there is something in gifts of the heart that merits preservation; and it is to be regretted that, when he died, these harps were broken up one after the other, and used as fire-wood by an ignorant follower of the family, who, on their removal to Cork for a temporary change of scene, was left in charge of the house.

The circumstances attending the death of Mr. Bunworth may be doubted by some; but there are still living credible witnesses who declare their authenticity, and who can be produced to attest most, if not all of the following particulars.

About a week previous to his dissolution, and early in the evening, a noise was heard at the hall-door resembling the shearing of sheep; but at the time no particular attention was paid to it. It was nearly eleven o'clock the same night, when Kavanagh, the herdsman, returned from Mallow, whither he had been sent in the afternoon for some medicine, and was observed by Miss Bunworth, to whom he delivered the parcel, to be much agitated. At this time, it must be observed, her father was by no means considered in danger.

"What is the matter, Kavanagh?" asked Miss Bunworth: but the poor fellow, with a bewildered look, only uttered, "The master, Miss—the master—he is going from us"; and, overcome with real grief, he burst into a flood of tears.

Miss Bunworth, who was a woman of strong nerve, inquired if any thing he had learned in Mallow induced him to suppose that her father was worse.

"No, Miss," said Kavanagh; "it was not in Mallow—"

"Kavanagh," said Miss Bunworth, with that stateliness of manner for which she is said to have been remarkable, "I fear you have been drinking, which I must say I did not expect at such a time as the present, when it was your duty to have kept yourself sober;—I thought you might have been trusted—what should we have done if you had broken the medicine bottle, or lost it? for the doctor said it was of the greatest consequence that your master should take it tonight. But I shall speak to you in the morning, when you are in a fitter state to understand what I say."

Kavanagh looked up with a stupidity of aspect which did not serve to remove the impression of his being drunk, as his eyes appeared heavy and dull after the flood of tears;—but his voice was not that of an intoxicated person.

"Miss," said he, "as I hope to receive mercy hereafter, neither bit nor sup has passed my lips since I left this house: but the master—"

"Speak softly," said Miss Bunworth; "he sleeps, and is going on as well as we could expect."

"Praise be to God for that, any way," replied Kavanagh; "but oh! miss, he is going from us surely—we will lose him—the master—we will lose him, we will lose him!" and he wrung his hands together.

"What is it you mean, Kavanagh?" asked Miss Bunworth.

"Is it mean?" said Kavanagh: "the Banshee has come for him, Miss; and 'tis not I alone who have heard her."

"'Tis an idle superstition," said Miss Bunworth.

"May be so," replied Kavanagh, as if the words "idle superstition" only sounded upon his ear without reaching his mind—"May be so," he continued;

"but as I came through the glen of Ballybeg, she was along with me keening and screeching and clapping her hands, by my side every step of the way, with her long white hair falling all about her shoulders, and I could hear her repeat the master's name every now and then, as plain as ever I heard it. When I came to the old abbey, she parted from me there, and turned into the pigeon-field next the *berrin* ground, and folding her cloak about her, down she sat under the tree that was struck by the lightning, and began keening so bitterly, that it went through one's heart to hear it."

"Kavanagh," said Miss Bunworth, who had, however, listened attentively to this remarkable relation, "my father is, I believe, better; and I hope will himself soon be up and able to convince you that all this is but your own fancy; nevertheless, I charge you not to mention what you have told me, for there is no occasion to frighten your fellow-servants with the story."

Mr. Bunworth gradually declined; but nothing particular occurred until the night previous to his death; that night both his daughters, exhausted from continued attendance and watching, were prevailed upon to seek some repose; and an elderly lady, a near relative and friend of the family, remained by the bedside of their father. The old gentleman then lay in the parlour, where he had been in the morning removed at his own request, fancying the change would afford him relief; and the head of his bed was placed close to the window. In a room adjoining sat some male friends, and as usual on like occasions of illness, in the kitchen many of the followers of the family had assembled.

The night was serene and moonlight—the sick man slept—and nothing broke the stillness of their melancholy watch, when the little party in the room adjoining the parlour, the door of which stood open, was suddenly roused by a sound at the window near the bed: a rose-tree grew outside the window, so close as to touch the glass; this was forced aside with some noise, and a low moaning was heard, accompanied by clapping of hands, as if of a female in deep affliction. It seemed as if the sound proceeded from a person holding her mouth close to the window. The lady who sat by the bed-side of Mr. Bunworth went into the adjoining room, and in a tone of alarm, inquired of the gentlemen there, if they had heard the Banshee? Sceptical of supernatural appearances, two of them rose hastily and went out to discover the cause of these sounds, which they also had distinctly heard. They walked all round the house, examining every spot of ground, particularly near the window from whence the voice had proceeded; the bed of earth beneath, in which the rose-tree was planted, had been recently dug, and the print of a footstep—if the tree had been forced aside by mortal hand—would have inevitably remained; but they could perceive no such impression; and an unbroken stillness reigned without.

Hoping to dispel the mystery, they continued their search anxiously along the road, from the straightness of which and the lightness of the night, they were enabled to see some distance around them; but all was silent and deserted, and they returned surprised and disappointed. How much more then were they astonished at learning that the whole time of their absence, those who remained within the house had heard the moaning and clapping of hands even louder and more distinct than before they had gone out; and no sooner was the door of the room closed on them, than they again heard the same mournful sounds! Every succeeding hour the sick man became worse, and as the first glimpse of the morning appeared, Mr. Bunworth expired.

The Fate of
Frank M'Kenna

WILLIAM CARLETON

There lived a man named M'Kenna at the hip of one of the mountainous hills which divide the county of Tyrone from that of Monaghan. This M'Kenna had two sons, one of whom was in the habit of tracing hares of a Sunday, whenever there happened to be a fall of snow. His father it seems had frequently remonstrated with him upon what he considered to be a violation of the Lord's day, as well as for his general neglect of mass. The young man, however, though otherwise harmless and inoffensive, was in this matter quite insensible to paternal reproof, and continued to trace whenever the avocations of labour would allow him. It so happened that upon a Christmas morning, I think in the year 1814, there was a deep fall of snow, and young M'Kenna, instead of going to mass, got down his cock-stick—which is a staff much thicker and heavier at one end than at the other—and prepared to set out on his favourite amusement. His father, seeing this, reproved him seriously, and insisted that he should attend prayers. His enthusiasm for the sport, however, was stronger than his love of religion, and he refused to be guided by his father's advice. The old man during the altercation got warm; and on finding that the son obstinately scorned his authority, he knelt down and prayed that if the boy persisted in following his own will, he might never return from the mountain unless as a corpse. The imprecation, which was certainly as harsh as it was impious and senseless, might have startled many a mind from a purpose that was, to say the least of it, at variance with religion and the respect due to a father. It had no effect, however, upon the son, who is said to have replied, that whether he ever returned or not, he was determined on going; and go accordingly he did. He was not, however, alone, for it appears that three or four of the neighbouring young men accompanied him. Whether their sport was good or otherwise, is not to the purpose, neither am I able to say; but the story goes, that towards the latter part of the day they started a larger and darker hare than any they had ever seen, and that she kept dodging on before them bit by bit, leading them to suppose that every succeeding cast of the cock-stick would bring her down. It was afterwards observed that she also led them into the recesses of the mountains, and that although they tried to turn her course homewards, they could not succeed in doing so. As evening advanced, the companions of M'Kenna began to feel the folly of pursuing her farther, and to perceive the danger of losing their way in the mountains should night or a snow-storm come upon them. They therefore proposed to give over the chase and return home; but M'Kenna would not hear of it. "If you wish to go home, you may," said he; "as for me, I'll never leave the hills till I have her with me." They begged and entreated of him to desist and return, but all to no purpose: he appeared to be what the Scotch call *fey*—that is, to act as if he were moved by some impulse that leads to death, and from the influence of which a man cannot withdraw himself. At length, on finding him invincibly obstinate, they left him pursuing the hare directly into the heart of the mountains, and returned to their respective homes.

In the meantime, one of the most terrible snow-storms ever remembered in that part of the country came on, and the consequence was, that the self-willed young man, who had equally trampled on the sanctions of religion and parental authority, was given over for lost. As soon as the tempest became still, the neighbours assembled in a body and proceeded to look for him. The snow, however, had fallen so heavily, that not a single mark of a footstep could be seen. Nothing but one wide waste of white undulating hills met the eye wherever it turned, and of M'Kenna no trace whatever was visible or could be found. His father now remembering the unnatural character of his imprecation, was nearly distracted; for although the body had not yet been found, still by everyone who witnessed the sudden rage of the storm and who knew the mountains, escape or survival was felt to be impossible. Every day for about a week large parties were out among the hill-ranges seeking him, but to no purpose. At length there came a thaw, and his body was found on a snow-wreath, lying in a supine posture within a circle which he had drawn around him with his cock-stick. His prayer-book lay opened upon his mouth, and his hat was pulled down so as to cover it and his face. It is unnecessary to say that the rumour of his death, and of the circumstances under which he left home, created a most extraordinary sensation in the country—a sensation that was the greater in proportion to the uncertainty occasioned by his not having been found either alive or dead. Some affirmed that he had crossed the mountains, and was seen in Monaghan; others, that he had been seen in Clones, in Emyvale, in Fivemiletown; but despite of all these agreeable reports, the melancholy truth was at length made clear by the appearance of the body as just stated.

Now, it so happened that the house nearest the spot where he lay was inhabited by a man named Daly, I think—but of name I am not certain—who was a herd or care-taker to Dr. Porter, then Bishop of Clogher. The situation of this house was the most lonely and desolate-looking that could be imagined. It was at least two miles distant from any human habitation, being surrounded by one wide and dreary waste of dark moor. By this house lay the route of those who had found the corpse, and I believe the door of it was borrowed for the purpose of conveying it home. Be this as it may, the family witnessed the melancholy procession as it passed slowly through the mountains, and when the place and circumstances are all considered, we may admit that to ignorant and superstitious people, whose minds even upon ordinary occasions were strongly affected by such matters, it was a sight calculated to leave behind it a deep, if not a terrible impression. Time soon proved that it did so.

An accident is said to have occurred at the funeral which I have alluded to in the "Midnight Mass," and which is certainly in fine keeping with the wild spirit of the whole melancholy event. When the procession had advanced to a place called Mullaghtinny, a large dark-coloured hare, which was instantly recognised, by those who had been out with him on the hills, as the identical one that led him to his fate, is said to have crossed the road about twenty yards or so before the coffin. The story goes, that a man struck it on the side with a stone, and that the blow, which would have killed any ordinary hare, not only did it no injury, but occasioned a sound to proceed from the body, resembling the hollow one emitted by an empty barrel when struck.

In the meantime the interment took place, and the sensation began like every other to die away in the natural progress of time, when, behold, a report ran abroad like wildfire that, to use the language of the people, "Frank M'Kenna was *appearing!*" Seldom indeed was the rumour of an apparition composed of materials so strongly calculated to win popular assent, or to baffle rational investigation. As every man is not a Hibbert, or a Nicolai, so will many, until such circumstances are made properly intelligible, continue to yield credence to testimony which would not convince the judgment on any other subject. The case in question furnished as fine a specimen of a true ghost-story, freed from any suspicion of imposture or design, as could be submitted to a philosopher; and yet, notwithstanding the array of apparent facts connected with it, nothing in the world is simpler or of easier solution.

One night, about a fortnight after his funeral, the daughter of Daly, the herd, a girl about fourteen, while lying in bed, saw what appeared to be the likeness of M'Kenna, who had been lost. She screamed out, and covering her head with the bed-clothes, told her father and mother that Frank M'Kenna was in the house. This alarming intelligence naturally produced great terror; still, Daly, who, notwithstanding his belief in such matters, possessed a good deal of moral courage, was cool enough to rise and examine the house, which consisted of only one apartment. This gave the daughter some courage, who, on finding that her father could not see him, ventured to look out, and she *then* could see nothing of him herself. She very soon fell asleep, and her father attributed what she saw to fear, or some accidental combination of shadows proceeding from the furniture, for it was a clear moon-light night. The light of the following day dispelled a great deal of their apprehensions, and comparatively little was thought of it until evening again advanced, when the fears of the daughter began to return. They appeared to be prophetic, for she said when night came that she knew he would appear again; and accordingly at the same hour he did so. This was repeated for several successive nights, until the girl, from the very hardihood of terror, began to become so familiarised to the spectre as to venture to address it.

"In the name of God!" she asked, "what is troubling you or why do you appear to me instead of to some of your own family or relations?"

The ghost's answer alone might settle the question involved in the authenticity of its appearance, being, as it was, an account of one of the most ludicrous missions that ever a spirit was despatched upon. "I'm not allowed," said he, "to spake to any of my friends, for I parted wid them in anger; but I'm come to tell you that they're quarrellin' about my breeches—a new pair that I got made for

Christmas day; an' as I was comin' up to trace in the mountains, I thought the ould ones 'ud do better, an' of coorse I didn't put the new pair an me. My raison for appearin'," he added, "is, that you may tell my friends that none of them is to wear them—they must be given in charity."

This serious and solemn intimation from the ghost was duly communicated to the family, and it was found that the circumstances were exactly as it had represented them. This of course was considered as sufficient proof of the truth of its mission. Their conversations now became not only frequent, but quite friendly and familiar. The girl became a favourite with the spectre, and the spectre on the other hand soon lost all his terrors in her eyes. He told her that whilst his friends were bearing home his body, the handspikes or poles on which they carried him had cut his back, and *occasioned him great pain!* The cutting of the back also was known to be true, and strengthened of course the truth and authenticity of their dialogues. The whole neighbourhood was now in a commotion with this story of the apparition, and persons incited by curiosity began to visit the girl in order to satisfy themselves of the truth of what they had heard. Everything, however, was corroborated, and the child herself, without any symptoms of anxiety or terror, artlessly related her conversations with the spirit. Hitherto their interviews had been all nocturnal, but now that the ghost found his footing made good, he put a hardy face on, and ventured to appear by day-light. The girl also fell into states of syncope, and while the fits lasted, long conversations with him upon the subject of God, the blessed Virgin, and Heaven, took place between them. He was certainly an excellent moralist, and gave the best, of advice. Swearing, drunkenness, theft, and every evil propensity of our nature, were declaimed against with a degree of spectral eloquence quite surprising. Common fame had now a topic dear to her heart, and never was a ghost made more of by his best friends, than she made of him. The whole country was in a tumult, and I well remember the crowds that flocked to the lonely little cabin in the mountains, now the scene of matters so interesting and important. Not a single day passed in which I should think from ten to twenty, thirty, or fifty persons were not present at these singular interviews. Nothing else was talked of, thought of, and, as I can well testify, dreamt of. I would myself have gone to Daly's, were it not for a confounded misgiving I had, that perhaps the ghost might take such a fancy of appearing to *me*, as he had taken to cultivate an intimacy with the girl; and it so happens, that when I see the face of an individual nailed down in the coffin—chilling and gloomy operation!—I experience no particular wish to look upon it again.

Many persons might imagine that the herd's daughter was acting the part of an impostor, by first originating and then continuing such a delusion. If any one, however, was an impostor, it was the ghost, and not the girl, as her ill health and wasted cheek might well testify. The appearance of M'Kenna continued to haunt her for months. The reader is aware that he was lost on Christmas day, or rather on the night of it, and I remember seeing her in the early part of the following summer, during which time she was still the victim of a diseased imagination. Everything in fact that could be done for her was done. They brought her to a priest named Donnelly, who lived down at Ballynaggart, for the purpose of getting her cured, as he had the reputation of performing cures of that kind. They brought her also to the doctors, who also did what they could for her; but all to no purpose. Her fits were longer and of more frequent occurrence; her appetite left her; and ere four months had elapsed, she herself looked as like a spectre as the ghost himself could do for the life of him.

It only now remains for me to mention the simple method of her cure, which was effected without either priest or doctor. It depended upon a word or two of advice given to her father by a very sensible man, who was in the habit of thinking on these matters somewhat above the superstitious absurdities of the people.

"If you wish your daughter to be cured," said he to her father, "leave the house you are now living in. Take her to some part of the country where she can have companions of her own class and state of life to mingle with; bring her away from the place altogether; for you may rest assured that so long as there are objects before her eyes to remind her of what happened, she will not mend on your hands."

The father, although he sat rent free, took this excellent advice, even at a sacrifice of some comfort: for nothing short of the temptation of easy circumstances could have induced any man to reside in so wild and remote a solitude. In the course of a few days he removed from it with his family, and came to reside amidst the cheerful aspect and enlivening intercourse of human life. The consequences were precisely as the man had told him. In the course of a few weeks the little girl began to find that the visits of the spectre were like those of angels, few and far between. She was sent to school, and what with the confidence derived from human society, and the substitution of new objects and images, she soon perfectly recovered, and ere long was thoroughly set free from the fearful creation of her own brain.

The spot where the body of M'Kenna was found is now marked by a little heap of stones, which has been collected since the melancholy event of his death. Every person who passes it throws a stone upon the heap; but why this old custom is practised, or what it means, I do not know, unless it be simply to mark the spot as a visible means of preserving the memory of the occurrence.

Daly's house, the scene of the supposed apparition, is now a shapeless ruin, which could scarcely be seen were it not for the green spot which was once a garden, and which now shines at a distance like an emerald, but with no agreeable or pleasing associations. It is a spot which no solitary school-boy will ever visit, nor indeed will the unflinching believer in the popular nonsense of ghosts wish to pass it without a companion. It is under any circumstances a gloomy and barren place, but when looked upon in connection with what we have just recited, it is lonely, desolate, and awful.

The Witch of Rathdowney

Anonymous

It was about eighty years ago, in the month of May, that a Roman Catholic clergyman, near Rathdowney, in the Queen's County, was awakened at midnight to attend a dying man in a distant part of the parish. The priest obeyed without a murmur, and having performed his duty to the expiring sinner, saw him depart this world before he left the cabin. As it was yet dark, the man who had called on the priest offered to accompany him home, but he refused, and set forward on his journey alone. He had not gone far, when the grey dawn began to appear over the hills, and he amused himself in contemplating the varied lovely scenes presented to the intelligent observer by the splendid breaking of a May-day morning. The eastern sky was streaked with all the magnificent shades of crimson, blue, and gold, so peculiar to "rosy May," and the brilliant morning star was shining as refulgently as if it had been created but that very hour. Every thing was hushed in calm repose, except the "merry lark," as Shakspeare calls her, which poised high in air, amid the fleecy, gold clouds, poured forth her matin hymn of praise and gratitude to the great Author of the Universe, or the wild, discordant cry of the heather-bleat from the adjacent morasses, or the irregular pattering of the large dew-drops, as they fell like globules of liquid silver from the stirless trees at either side of the road. The good priest was highly enraptured with the beauty of the scene, and rode on, now gazing intently at every surrounding object, and again cutting with his whip at the bats and big beautiful night-flies which flitted ever and anon from hedge to hedge across his lonely way. Thus engaged, he journeyed on slowly, until the nearer approach of sunrise began to render objects completely discernible, when he dismounted from his horse, and slipping his arm out in the rein, and drawing forth his "Breviary" from his pocket, he commenced reading his "morning office" as he walked leisurely along.

He had not proceeded very far, when he observed his horse, a very spirited animal, endeavouring to stop on the road, and gazing intently into a field on one side of the way where there were three or four cows grazing. However, he did not pay any particular attention to this circumstance, but went on a little farther, when the horse suddenly lunged with great violence, and endeavoured to break away by force. The priest with great difficulty succeeded in restraining him, and, looking at him more closely, observed him shaking from head to foot, and sweating profusely. He now stood calmly, and refused to move from where he was, nor could threats or intreaty induce him to proceed. The father was greatly astonished, but recollecting to have often heard of horses labouring under affright being induced to go by blindfolding them, he took out his handkerchief and tied it across his eyes. He then mounted, and, striking him gently, he went forward without reluctance, but still sweating and trembling violently. They had not gone far, when they arrived opposite a narrow path or bridle-way, flanked at either side by a tall, thick hedge, which led from the high road to the field where the cows were grazing. The priest happened by chance to look into the lane, and saw a spectacle which made the blood curdle in his veins. It was the legs of a man from the hips downwards, without head or body, trotting up the avenue at a smart pace. The good father was very much alarmed, but, being a man of strong nerve, he resolved, come what might, to stand, and be further acquainted with this singular spectre. He accordingly stood, and so did the headless apparition, as if afraid to approach him. The priest, observing this, pulled back a little from the entrance of the avenue, and the phantom again resumed its progress. It soon arrived on the road, and the priest now had sufficient opportunity to view it minutely. It wore yellow buckskin breeches, tightly fastened at the knees with green ribbon; it had neither shoes nor stockings on, and its legs were covered with long, red hairs, and all full of wet, blood, and clay, apparently contracted in its progress through the thorny hedges. The priest, although very much alarmed, felt eager to examine the phantom, and for this purpose he determined to screw his courage to the sticking point, and to summon all his philosophy to enable him to speak to it. The ghost was now a little a-head, pursuing its march at its usual brisk trot, and the priest urged on his horse speedily until he came up with it, and thus addressed it:—

"Hilloa, friend, who art thou, or whither art thou going so early?"

The hideous spectre made no reply, but uttered a fierce and superhuman growl or "umph."

"A fine morning for ghosts to wander abroad," again said the priest.

Another "Umph" was the reply.

"Why don't you speak?"

"Umph."

"You don't seem disposed to be very loquacious this morning."

"Umph" again.

The good man began to feel irritated at the obstinate silence of his unearthly visitor, and said, with some warmth—

"In the name of all that's sacred, I command you to answer me, who art thou, or where art thou travelling?"

Another "Umph" more loud and more angry than before was the only reply.

"Perhaps," said the father, " a taste of whipcord might render you a little more communicative"; and so saying, he struck the apparition a heavy blow with his whip on the breech.

The phantom uttered a wild and unearthly yell, and fell forward on the road, and what was the priest's astonishment, when he perceived the whole place running over with milk. He was struck dumb with amazement; the prostrate phantom still continued to eject vast quantities of milk from every part; the priest's head swam, his eyes got dizzy; a stupor came all over him for some minutes, and on his recovering, the frightful spectre had vanished, and in its stead he found stretched on the road, and half drowned in milk, the form of Sarah Kennedy, an old woman of the neighbourhood, who had been long notorious in that district for her witchcraft and superstitious practices, and it was now discovered that she had, by infernal aid, assumed that monstrous shape, and was employed that morning in sucking the cows of the village. Had a volcano burst forth at his feet, he could not be more astonished; he gazed awhile in silent amazement—the old woman groaning, and writhing convulsively.

"Sarah," said he, at length, " I have long admonished you to repent of your evil ways, but you were deaf to my intreaties, and now, wretched woman, you are surprised in the midst of your crime."

"Oh, father, father," shouted the unfortunate woman, "can you do nothing to save me? I am lost; hell is open for me, and legions of devils surround me this moment, waiting to carry my soul to perdition."

The priest had not power to reply; the old wretch's pains increased; her body swelled to an immense size; her eyes flashed as if in fire, her face was black as night, her entire form writhed in a thousand different contortions; her outcries were appalling, her face sunk, her eyes closed, and in a few minutes she expired in the most exquisite tortures.

The priest departed homewards, and called at the next cabin to give notice of the strange circumstances. The remains of Sarah Kennedy were removed to her cabin, situated at the edge of a small wood at a little distance. She had long been a resident in that neighbourhood, but still she was a stranger, and came there, no one knew from whence. She had no relation in that country but one daughter, now advanced in years, who resided with her. She kept one cow, but sold more butter, it was said, than any farmer in the parish, and it was generally suspected that she acquired it by devilish agency, as she never made a secret of being intimately acquainted with sorcery and fairyism. She professed the Roman Catholic religion, but never complied with the practices enjoined by that church, and her remains were denied Christian sepulture, and were buried in a sand-pit near her own cabin.

On the evening of her burial, the villagers assembled and burned her cabin to the earth; her daughter made her escape, and never after returned.

The Priest's Soul

LADY WILDE

In former days there were great schools in Ireland where every sort of learning was taught to the people, and even the poorest had more knowledge at that time than many a gentleman has now. But as to the priests, their learning was above all, so that the fame of Ireland went over the whole world, and many kings from foreign lands used to send their sons all the way to Ireland to be brought up in the Irish schools.

Now at this time there was a little boy learning at one of them who was a wonder to every one for his cleverness. His parents were only labouring people, and of course very poor; but young as he was, and poor as he was, no king's or lord's son could come up to him in learning. Even the masters were put to shame, for when they were trying to teach him he would tell them something they never heard of before, and show them their ignorance. One of his great triumphs was in argument; and he would go on till he proved to you that black was white, and then when you gave in, for no one could beat him in talk, he would turn round and show you that white was black, or may be that there was no colour at all in the world. When he grew up his poor father and mother were so proud of him that they resolved to make him a priest, which they did at last, though they nearly starved themselves to get the money. Well, such another learned man was not in Ireland, and he was as great in argument as ever, so that no one could stand before him. Even the Bishops tried to talk to him, but he showed them at once they knew nothing at all.

Now there were no schoolmasters in those times but it was the priests taught the people; and as this man was the cleverest in Ireland all the foreign kings sent their sons to him as long as he had house-room to give them. So he grew very proud, and began to forget how low he had been, and worst of all, even to forget God, who had made him what he was. And the pride of arguing got hold of him, so that from one thing to another he went on to prove that there was no Purgatory, and then no Hell, and then no Heaven, and then no God; and at last that men had no souls, but were no more than a dog or a cow, and when they died there was an end of them. "Who ever saw a soul?" he would say. "If you can show me one, I will believe." No one could make any answer to this; and at last they all came to believe that as there was no other world, every one might do what they liked in this; the priest setting the example, for he took a beautiful young girl to wife. But as no priest or bishop in the whole land could be got to marry them, he was obliged to read the service over for himself. It was a great scandal, yet no one dared to say a word, for all the kings' sons were on his side, and would have slaughtered any one who tried to prevent his wicked goings-on. Poor boys! they all believed in him, and thought every word he said was the truth. In this way his notions began to spread about, and the whole world was going to the bad, when one night an angel came down from Heaven, and told the priest he had but twenty-four hours to live. He began to tremble, and asked for a little more time.

But the angel was stiff, and told him that could not be.

"What do you want time for, you sinner?" he asked.

"Oh, sir, have pity on my poor soul!" urged the priest.

"Oh, ho! You have a soul, then," said the angel. "Pray, how did you find that out?"

"It has been fluttering in me ever since you appeared," answered the priest. "What a fool I was not to think of it before."

"A fool indeed," said the angel. "What good was all your learning, when it could not tell you that you had a soul?"

"Ah, my lord," said the priest, "if I am to die, tell me how soon I may be in Heaven?"

"Never," replied the angel. "You denied there was a Heaven."

"Then, my lord, may I go to Purgatory?"

"You denied Purgatory also; you must go straight to Hell," said the angel.

"But, my lord, I denied Hell also," answered the priest, "so you can't send me there either." The angel was a little puzzled.

"Well," said he, "I'll tell you what I can do for you. You may either live now on earth for a hundred years enjoying every pleasure, and then be cast into Hell for ever; or you may die in twenty-four hours in the most horrible torments, and pass through Purgatory, there to remain till the Day of Judgment, if only you can find some one person that believes, and through his belief mercy will be vouchsafed to you and your soul will be saved."

The priest did not take five minutes to make up his mind.

"I will have death in the twenty-four hours," he said, "so that my soul may be saved at last."

On this the angel gave him directions as to what he was to do, and left him.

Then, immediately, the priest entered the large room where all his scholars and the kings' sons were seated, and called out to them—

"Now, tell me the truth, and let none fear to contradict me. Tell me what is your belief. Have men souls?"

"Master," they answered, "once we believed that men had souls; but, thanks to your teaching, we believe so no longer. There is no Hell, and no Heaven, and no God. This is our belief, for it is thus you taught us."

Then the priest grew pale with fear and cried out—"Listen! I taught you a lie. There is a God, and man has an immortal soul, I believe now all I denied before."

But the shouts of laughter that rose up drowned the priest's voice, for they thought he was only trying them for argument.

"Prove it, master," they cried, "prove it. Who has ever seen God? Who has ever seen the soul?"

And the room was stirred with their laughter.

The priest stood up to answer them, but no word could he utter; all his eloquence, all his powers of argument had gone from him, and he could do nothing but wring his hands and cry out—

"There is a God! there is a God! Lord have mercy on my soul!"

And they all began to mock him, and repeat his own words that he had taught them—

"Show him to us; show us your God."

And he fled from them groaning with agony, for he saw that none believed, and how then could his soul be saved? But he thought next of his wife.

"She will believe," he said to himself. "Women never give up God."

And he went to her; but she told him that she believed only what he taught her, and that a good wife should believe in her husband first, and before and above all things in heaven or earth.

Then despair came on him, and he rushed from the house and began to ask every one he met if they believed. But the same answer came from one and all—"We believe only what you have taught us," for his doctrines had spread far and wide through the county.

Then he grew half mad with fear, for the hours were passing. And he flung himself down on the ground in a lonesome spot, and wept and groaned in terror, for the time was coming fast when he must die.

Just then a little child came by.

"God save you kindly," said the child to him.

The priest started up.

"Child, do you believe in God?" he asked.

"I have come from a far country to learn about Him," said the child. "Will your honour direct me to the best school that they have in these parts?"

"The best school and the best teacher is close by," said the priest, and he named himself.

"Oh, not to that man," answered the child, "for I am told he denies God, and Heaven, and Hell, and even that man has a soul, because we can't see it; but I would soon put him down."

The priest looked at him earnestly. "How?" he inquired.

"Why," said the child, " I would ask him if he believed he had life to show me his life."

"But he could not do that, my child," said the priest. "Life cannot be seen; we have it, but it is invisible."

"Then if we have life, though we cannot see it, we may also have a soul, though it is invisible," answered the child.

When the priest heard him speak these words he fell down on his knees before him, weeping for joy, for now he knew his soul was safe; he had met at last one that believed. And he told the child his whole story: all his wickedness, and pride, and blasphemy against the great God; and how the angel had come to him and told him of the only way in which he could be saved, through the faith and prayers of some one that believed.

"Now then," he said to the child, "take this penknife and strike it into my breast, and go on stabbing the flesh until you see the paleness of death on my face. Then watch—for a living thing will soar up from my body as I die, and you will then know that my soul has ascended to the presence of God. And when you see this thing, make haste and run to my school and call on all my scholars to come and see that the soul of their master has left the body, and that all he taught them was a lie, for that there is a God who punishes sin, and a Heaven and a Hell, and that man has an immortal soul, destined for eternal happiness or misery."

"I will pray," said the child," to have courage to do this work."

And he kneeled down and prayed. Then when he rose up he took the penknife and struck it into the priest's heart, and struck and struck again till all the flesh was lacerated; but still the priest lived though the agony was horrible, for he could not die until the twenty-four hours had expired. At last the agony seemed to cease, and the stillness of death settled on his face. Then the child, who was watching, saw a beautiful living creature, with four snow white wings, mount from the dead man's body into the air and go fluttering round his head.

So he ran to bring the scholars; and when they saw it they all knew it was the soul of their master, and they watched with wonder and awe until it passed from sight into the clouds.

And this was the first butterfly that was ever seen in Ireland; and now all men know that the butterflies are the souls of the dead waiting for the moment when they may enter Purgatory, and so pass through torture to purification and peace.

But the schools of Ireland were quite deserted after that time, for people said, What is the use of going so far to learn when the wisest man in all Ireland did not know if he had a soul till he was near losing it; and was only saved at last through the simple belief of a little child?

The Three Wishes

WILLIAM CARLETON

In ancient times there lived a man called Billy Dawson, and he was known to be a great rogue. They say he was descended from the family of the Dawsons, which was the reason, I suppose, of his carrying their name upon him.

Billy, in his youthful days, was the best hand at doing nothing in all Europe; devil a mortal could come next or near him at idleness; and, in consequence of his great practice that way, you may be sure that if any man could make a fortune by it he would have done it.

Billy was the only son of his father, barring two daughters; but they have nothing to do with the story I'm telling you. Indeed it was kind father and grandfather for Billy to be handy at the knavery as well as at the idleness; for it was well known that not one of their blood ever did an honest act, except with a roguish intention. In short, they were altogether a *dacent* connexion, and a credit to the name. As for Billy, all the villany of the family, both plain and ornamental, came down to him by way of legacy; for it so happened that the father, in spite of all his cleverness, had nothing but his roguery to *lave* him.

Billy, to do him justice, improved the fortune he got: every day advanced him farther into dishonesty and poverty, until, at the long run, he was acknowledged on all hands to be the completest swindler and the poorest vagabond in the whole parish.

Billy's father, in his young days, had often been forced to acknowledge the inconvenience of not having a trade, in consequence of some nice point in law, called the "Vagrant Act," that sometimes troubled him. On this account he made up his mind to give Bill an occupation, and he accordingly bound him to a blacksmith; but whether Bill was to *live* or *die* by *forgery* was a puzzle to his father,—though the neighbours said that *both* was most likely. At all events, he was put apprentice to a smith for seven years, and a hard card his master had to play in managing him. He took the proper method, however, for Bill was so lazy and roguish that it would vex a saint to keep him in order.

"Bill," says his master to him one day that he had been sunning himself about the ditches, instead of minding his business, "Bill, my boy, I'm vexed to the heart to see you in such a bad state of health. You're very ill with that complaint called an *All-overness*; however," says, he, "I think I can cure you. Nothing will bring you about but three or four sound doses, every day, of a medicine called 'the oil o' the hazel.' Take the first dose now" says he; and he immediately banged him, with a hazel cudgel until Bill's bones ached for a week afterwards.

"If you were my son," said his master, "I tell you, that, as long as I could get a piece of advice growing convenient in the hedges, I'd have you a different youth from what you are. If working was a sin, Bill, not an innocenter boy ever broke bread than you would be. Good people's scarce you think; but however that may be, I throw it out as a hint, that you must take your medicine till you're cured, whenever you happen to get unwell in the same way."

From this out he kept Bill's nose to the grinding-stone, and whenever his complaint returned, he never failed to give him a hearty dose for his improvement.

In the course of time, however, Bill was his own man and his own master; but it would puzzle a saint to know whether the master or the man was the more precious youth in the eyes of the world.

He immediately married a wife, and devil a doubt of it, but if *he* kept *her* in whiskey and sugar, *she* kept *him* in hot water. Bill drank and she drank; Bill fought and she fought; Bill was idle and she was idle; Bill whacked her and she whacked Bill. If Bill gave her one black eye, she gave him another; *just to keep herself in countenance.* Never was there a blessed pair so well met; and a beautiful sight it was

to see them both at breakfast-time blinking at each
other across the potato-basket, Bill with his right
eye black, and she with her left.

In short, they were the talk of the whole town:
and to see Bill of a morning staggering home
drunk, his shirt sleeves rolled up on his smutted
arms, his breast open, and an old tattered leather
apron, with one corner tucked up under his belt,
singing one minute, and fighting with his wife the
next;—she, reeling beside him, with a discoloured
eye, as aforesaid, a dirty ragged cap on one side of
her head, a pair of Bill's old slippers on her feet,
a squalling child on her arm,—now cuffing and
dragging Bill, and again kissing and hugging him!
yes it was a pleasant picture to see this loving pair
in such a state!

This might do for a while, but it could not last.
They were idle, drunken, and ill-conducted; and it
was not to be supposed that they would get a far-
thing candle on their words. They were of course
dhruv to great straits; and faith, they soon found
that their fighting, and drinking, and idleness
made them the laughing-sport of the neighbours;
but neither brought food to their *childhre,* put a
coat upon their backs, nor satisfied their landlord
when he came to look for his own. Still the never
a one of Bill but was a funny fellow with strangers,
though, as we said, the greatest rogue unhanged.

One day he was standing against his own anvil,
completely in a brown study,—being brought to

his wit's end how to make out a breakfast for the family. The wife was scolding and cursing in the house, and the naked creatures of childhre squalling about her knees for food. Bill was fairly at an amplush, and knew not where or how to turn himself, when a poor withered old beggar came into the forge, tottering on his staff. A long white beard fell from his chin, and he looked so thin and hungry that you might blow him, one would think, over the house. Bill at this moment had been brought to his senses by distress, and his heart had a touch of pity towards the old man; for, on looking at him a second time, he clearly saw starvation and sorrow in his face. "God save you, honest man!" said Bill. The old man gave a sigh, and raising himself with great pain, on his staff, he looked at Bill in a very beseeching way.

"Musha, God save you kindly!" says he; "maybe you could give a poor, hungry, helpless ould man a mouthful of something to ait? You see yourself I'm not able to work; if I was, I'd scorn to be beholding to any one."

"Faith, honest man," said Bill, "if you knew who you're speaking to, you'd as soon ask a monkey for a churn-staff as me for either mate or money. There's not a blackguard in the three kingdoms so fairly on the *shaughran* as I am for both the one and the other. The wife within is sending the curses thick and heavy on me, and the childhre's playing the cat's melody to keep her in comfort. Take my word for it, poor man, if I had either mate or money I'd help you, for I know particularly well what it is to want them at the present spaking; an empty sack won't stand, neighbour."

So far Bill told him truth. The good thought was in his heart, because he found himself on a footing with the beggar; and nothing brings down pride, or softens the heart, like feeling what it is to want.

"Why you are in a worse state than I am," said the old man; "you have a family to provide for, and I have only myself to support."

"You may kiss the book on that, my old worthy," replied Bill; "but come, what I can do for you I will; plant yourself up here beside the fire, and I'll give it a blast or two of my bellows that will warm the old blood in your body. It's a cold, miserable, snowy day, and a good heat will be of service."

"Thank you kindly," said the old man; "I *am* cold, and a warming at your fire will do me good, sure enough. Oh, it *is* a bitter, bitter day, God bless it!"

He then sat down, and Bill blew a rousing blast that soon made the stranger edge back from the heat. In a short time he felt quite comfortable, and when the numbness was taken out of his joints, he buttoned himself up and prepared to depart.

"Now," says he to Bill, "you hadn't the food to give me, but *what you could you did.* Ask any three wishes you choose, and be they what they may, take my word for it, they shall be granted."

Now, the truth is, that Bill, though he believed himself a great man in point of 'cuteness, wanted, after all, a full quarter of being square; for there is always a great difference between a wise man and a knave. Bill was so much of a rogue that he could not, for the blood of him, ask an honest wish, but stood scratching his head in a puzzle.

"Three wishes!" said he. "Why, let me see—did you say *three?*"

"Ay," replied the stranger, "three wishes—that was what I said."

"Well," said Bill, "here goes,—aha!—let me alone, my old worthy!—faith I'll over-reach the parish, if what you say is true. I'll cheat them in dozens, rich and poor, old and young: let me alone, man,—I have it here"; and he tapped his forehead with great glee. "Faith, you're the sort to meet of a frosty morning, when a man wants his breakfast; and I'm sorry that I have neither money nor credit to get a bottle of whiskey, that we might take our *morning* together."

"Well, but let us hear the wishes," said the old man; "my time is short, and I cannot stay much longer."

"Do you see this sledge hammer?" said Bill; "I wish, in the first place, that whoever takes it up in their hands may never be able to lay it down till I give them lave; and that whoever begins to sledge with it may never stop sledging till it's my pleasure to release him."

"Secondly—I have an arm-chair, and I wish that whoever sits down in it may never rise out of it till they have my consent."

"And thirdly—that whatever money I put into my purse, nobody may have power to take it out of it but myself!"

"You devil's rip!" says the old man in a passion, shaking his staff across Bill's nose, "why did you not ask something that would sarve you both here and hereafter? Sure it's as common as the market-cross, that there's not a vagabone in his Majesty's dominions stands more in need of both."

"Oh! by the elevens," said Bill, "I forgot that altogether! Maybe you'd be civil enough to let me change one of them? The sorra purtier wish ever was made than I'll make, if you'll give me another chance."

"Get out, you reprobate," said the old fellow, still in a passion. "Your day of grace is past. Little you knew who was speaking to you all this time. I'm St. Moroky, you blackguard, and I gave you an opportunity of doing something for yourself and your family; but you neglected it, and now your fate is cast, you dirty, bog-trotting profligate. Sure it's well known what you are! Aren't you a byword in every body's mouth, you and your scold of a wife? By this and by that, if ever you happen to come across me again, I'll send you to where you won't freeze, you villain!"

He then gave Bill a rap of his cudgel over the head, and laid him at his length beside the bellows, kicked a broken coal-scuttle out of his way, and left the forge in a fury.

When Billy recovered himself from the effects of the blow, and began to think on what had happened, he could have quartered himself with vexation for not asking great wealth as one of the wishes at least; but now the die was cast on him, and he could only make the most of the three he pitched upon.

He now bethought him now he might turn them to the best account, and here his cunning came to his aid. He began by sending for his wealthiest neighbours on pretence of business; and when he got them under his roof, he offered them the arm-chair to sit down in. He now had them safe, nor could all the art of man relieve them except worthy Bill was willing. Bill's plan was to make the best bargain he could before he released his prisoners; and let him alone for knowing how to make their purses bleed. There wasn't a wealthy man in the country he did not fleece. The parson of the parish bled heavily; so did the lawyer; and a rich attorney, who had retired from practice, swore that the court of Chancery itself was paradise compared to Bill's chair.

This was all very good for a time. The fame of his chair, however, soon spread; so did that of his sledge. In a short time neither man, woman, nor child, would darken his door; all avoided him and his fixtures as they would a spring-gun or man-trap.

Bill, so long as he fleeced his neighbours, never wrought a hand's turn; so that when his money was out, he found himself as badly off as ever. In addition to all this, his character was fifty times worse than before; for it was the general belief that he had dealings with the old boy. Nothing now could exceed his misery, distress, and ill temper. The wife and he and their children all fought among one another. Every body hated them, cursed them, and avoided them. The people thought they were acquainted with more than Christian people ought to know. This, of course, came to Bill's ears, and it vexed him very much.

One day he was walking about the fields, thinking of how he could raise the wind once more; the day was dark, and he found himself, before he stopped, in the bottom of a lonely glen covered by great bushes that grew on each side. "Well," thought he, when every other means of raising money failed him, "it's reported that I'm in league with the old-boy, and as it's a folly to have the name of the connexion without the profit, I'm ready to make a bargain with him any day;—so," said he, raising his voice, "Nick, you sinner, if you be convanient and willing, why stand out here; show your best leg,—here's your man."

The words were hardly out of his mouth, when a dark sober-looking old gentleman, not unlike a lawyer, walked up to him. Bill looked at the foot and saw the hoof.—"Morrow, Nick," says Bill.

"Morrow, Bill," says Nick. "Well, Bill, what's the news?"

"Devil a much myself hears of late," says Bill, "is there any thing *fresh* below?"

"I can't exactly say, Bill; I spend little of my time down now; the Tories are in office, and my hands are consequently too full of business here to pay much attention to any thing else."

"A fine place this, sir," says Bill, "to take a constitutional walk in; when I want an appetite I often come this way myself,—hem! *High* feeding is very bad without exercise."

"High feeding! Come, come, Bill, you know you didn't taste a morsel these four-and-twenty hours."

"You know that's a bounce, Nick. I eat a breakfast this morning that would put a stone of flesh on you, if you only smelt at it."

"No matter; this is not to the purpose. What's that you were muttering to yourself awhile ago? If you want to come to the brunt, here I'm for you."

"Nick" said Bill, "you're complate; you want nothing barring a pair of Brian O'Lynn's breeches."

Bill, in fact, was bent on making his companion open the bargain, because he had often heard, that in that case, with proper care on his own part, he might defeat him in the long run. The other, however, was his match.

"What was the nature of Brian's garment," inquired Nick.—"Why, you know the song," said Bill—

"Brian O'Lynn had no breeches to wear.
  So he got a sheep's skin for to make him
      a pair;
  With the fleshy side out and the woolly
      side in,
  They'll be pleasant and *cool*, says Brian
      O'Lynn.

A *cool* pare would sarve you, Nick."

"You're mighty waggish to-day, misther Dawson."

"And good right I have," said Bill; "I'm a man snug and well to do in the world; have lots of money, plenty of good eating and drinking, and what more need a man wish for?"

"True," said the other; "in the meantime it's rather odd that so respectable a man should not have six inches of unbroken cloth in his apparel. You are as naked a tatter-demallion as I ever laid my eyes on; in full dress for a party of scare-crows, William."

"That's my own fancy, Nick; I don't work at my trade like a gentleman. This is my forge dress, you know."

"Well, but what did you summon me here for?" said the other; "you may as well speak out I tell you; for, my good friend, unless *you* do *I* shan't. Smell that."

"I smell more than that," said Bill; "and by the way, I'll thank you to give me the windy side of you—curse all sulphur I say. There, that's what I call an improvement in my condition. But as you *are* so stiff," says Bill, "why, the short and the long of it is—that—hem—you see I'm—tut—sure you know I have a thriving trade of my own, and that if I like I needn't be at a loss; but in the manetime I'm rather in a kind of a so—so—don't you *take?*"

And Bill winked knowingly, hoping to trick him into the first proposal.

"You must speak above-board, my friend," says the other; "I'm a man of few words, blunt and honest. If you have anything to say, be plain. Don't think I can be losing my time with such a pitiful rascal as you are."

"Well," says Bill, "I want money, then, and am ready to come into terms. What have you to say to that, Nick?"

"Let me see—let me look at you," says his companion, turning him about. "Now, Bill, in the first place, are you not as finished a scare-crow as ever stood upon two legs?"

"I play second fiddle to you there again," says Bill.

"There you stand with the blackguards' coat of arms quartered under your eye, and—

"Don't make little of *blackguards*," said Bill, "nor spake disparagingly of *your own* crest."

"Why, what would you bring, you brazen rascal, if you were fairly put up at auction?"

"Faith, I'd bring more bidders than you would," said Bill, "if you were to go off at auction to-morrow. I tell you they should bid *downwards* to come to your value, Nicholas. We have no coin *small* enough to purchase you."

"Well, no matter," said Nick, "If you are willing to be mine at the expiration of seven years, I will give you more money than ever the rascally breed of you was worth."

"Done!" said Bill; "but no disparagement to my family, in the meantime; so down with the hard cash, and don't be a *neger.*"

The money was accordingly paid down! but as nobody was present, except the giver and receiver, the amount of what Bill got was never known.

"Won't you give me a luck-penny?" said the old gentleman.

"Tut," said Billy, "so prosperous an old fellow as you cannot want it; however, bad luck to you, with all my heart! and it's rubbing grease to a fat pig to say so. Be off now, or I'll commit suicide on you. Your absence is a cordial to most people, you infernal old profligate. You have injured my morals even for the short time you have been with me; for I don't find myself so virtuous as I was."

"Is that your gratitude, Billy?"

"Is it gratitude *you* speak of, man ? I wonder you don't blush when you name it. However, when you come again, if you bring a third eye in your head you will see what I mane, Nicholas, ahagur."

The old gentleman, as Bill spoke, hopped across the ditch, on his way to *Downing*-street, where of late 'tis thought he possesses much influence.

Bill now began by degrees to show off; but still wrought a little at his trade to blindfold the neighbours. In a very short time, however, he became great man. So long indeed as he was a *poor* rascal, no decent person would speak to him; even the proud serving-men at the "Big House " would turn up their noses at him. And he well deserved to be made little of by others, because he was mean enough to make little of himself. But when it was seen and known that he had oceans of money, it was wonderful to think, although he was *now* a greater blackguard than ever, how those who despised him before, egan to come round him and court his company. Bill, however, had neither sense nor spirit to make those sunshiny friends know their distance; not he—instead of that he was proud to be seen in decent company, and so long as the money lasted, it was, "hail fellow well met," between himself and every fair-faced *spunger* who had a horse under him, a decent coat to his back, and a good appetite to eat his dinners. With riches and all, Bill was the same man still; but, somehow or other, there is a great difference between a rich profligate and a poor one, and Bill found it so to his cost in *both* cases.

Before half the seven years was passed, Bill had his carriage, and his equipages; was hand and glove with my Lord This, and my Lord That; kept hounds and hunters; was the first sportsman at the Curragh; patronized every boxing ruffian he could pick up; and betted night and day on cards, dice, and horses. Bill, in short, *should* be a blood, and except he did all this, he could not presume to mingle with the fashionable bloods of his time.

It's an old proverb, however, that "what is got over the devil's back is sure to go off under it; and in Bill's case this proved true. In short, the old boy himself could not supply him with money so fast as he made it fly; it was "come easy, go easy," with Bill, and so sign was on it, before he came within two years of his time he found his purse empty.

And now came the value of his summer friends to be known. When it was discovered that the cash was no longer flush with him—that stud, and carriage, and hounds were going to the hammer—whish! off they went, friends, relations, pot-companions, din-ner-eaters, black-legs and all, like a flock of crows that had smelt gunpowder. Down Bill soon went, week after week, and day after day, until at last, he was obliged to put on the leather apron and take to the hammer again; and not only that, for as no experience could make him wise, he once more began his tap-room brawls, his quarrels with Judy, and took to his "high feeding" at the dry potatoes and salt. Now, too, came the cutting tongues of all who knew him, like razors upon him. Those that he scorned because they were poor and himself rich, now paid him back his own with interest; and those that he measured himself with, because they were rich, and who only countenanced him in consequence of his wealth, gave him the hardest word in their cheeks. The devil mend him! He deserved it all, and more if he had got it.

Bill, however, who was a hardened sinner, never fretted himself down an ounce of flesh by what was said to him, or of him. Not he; he cursed, and fought, and swore, and schemed away as usual, taking in every one he could; and surely none could match him at villany of all sorts and sizes.

At last the seven years became expired, and Bill was one morning sitting in his forge, sober and hungry, the wife cursing him; and the childhre squaling, as before; he was thinking how he might defraud some honest neighbour out of a breakfast to stop their mouths and his own too, when who walks in to him but old Nick, to demand his bargain.

"Morrow, Bill!" says he with a sneer.

"The devil welcome you!" says Bill; "but you have a fresh memory."

"A bargain's a bargain between two *honest* men, any day," says Satan; "when I speak of *honest* men, I mean *yourself* and *me*, Bill"; and he put his tongue in his cheek to make game of the unfortunate rogue he had come for.

"Nick, my worthy fellow," said Bill, "have bowels; you wouldn't do a shabby thing; you wouldn't disgrace your own character by putting more weight upon a falling man. You know what it is to get a *come down* yourself, my worthy: so just keep your toe in your pump, and walk off with yourself somewhere else. A *cool* walk will sarve you better than my company, Nicholas."

"Bill, it's no use in shirking"; said his friend, "your swindling tricks may enable you to cheat others, but you won't cheat *me,* I guess. You want nothing to make you perfect in your way but to travel; and travel you shall under my guidance, Billy. No, no—*I'm* not to be swindled my good fellow. I have rather a—a—better opinion of myself, Mr. D. than to think that you could outwit one Nicholas Clutie, Esq.—ehem!"

"You may sneer, you sinner," replied Bill; "but I tell you that I have outwitted men who could buy and sell you to your face. Despair, you villain, when I tell you that *no attorney* could stand before me."

Satan's countenance got blank when he heard this; he wriggled and fidgetted about, and appeared to be not quite comfortable.

"In that case, then," says he, "the sooner I *deceive* you the better; so turn out for the *Low Countries.*"

"Is it come to that in earnest?" said Bill, "and are you going to act the rascal at the long run?"

"'Pon honour, Bill."

"Have patience, then, you sinner, till I finish this horse-shoe—it's the last of a set I'm finishing for one of your friend the attorney's horses.

And here; Nick, I hate idleness, you know it's the mother of mischief, take this sledge-hammer, and give a dozen strokes or so, till I get it out of hands, and then here's with you, since it must be so."

He then gave the bellows a puff that blew half a peck of dust in Club-foot's face, whipped out the red-hot iron, and set Satan sledging away for the bare life.

"Faith," says Bill to him, when the shoe was finished, "it's a thousand pities ever the sledge should be out of your hand; the great *Parra Gow* was a child to you at sledging, you're such an able tyke. Now just exercise yourself till I bid the wife and childhre good-bye, and then I'm off."

Out went Bill, of course, without the slightest notion of coming back; no more than Nick had that he could not give up the sledging, and indeed neither could he, but was forced to work away as if he was sledging for a wager. This was just what Bill wanted. He was now compelled to sledge on until it was Bill's pleasure to release him; and so we leave him very industriously employed, while we look after the worthy who outwitted him.

In the meantime, Bill broke cover, and took to the country at large; wrought a little journey-work wherever he could get it, and in this way went from one place to another, till in the course of a month, he walked back very coolly into his own forge, to see how things went on in his absence. There he found Satan in a rage, the perspiration pouring from him in torrents, hammering with might and main upon the naked anvil. Bill calmly leaned his back against the wall, placed his hat upon the side of his head, put his hands into his breeches pockets, and began to whistle *Shaun Gow's* hornpipe. At length he says in a very quiet and good-humoured way—

"Morrow, Nick!"

"Oh!" says Nick, still hammering away—"Oh! you double-distilled villain (hech!), may the most refined, ornamental (hech!), double-rectified, super-extra, and original (hech!) collection of curses that ever was gathered (hech!) into a single nosegay of ill fortune (hech!), shine in the button-hole of your conscience (hech!) while your name is Bill Dawson! I denounce you (hech!) as a double-milled villain, a finished, hot-pressed knave (hech!), in comparison of whom all the other knaves I ever knew (hech!), attorneys included, are honest men. I brand you (hech!) as the pearl of cheats, a tip-top take-in (hech!) I denounce you, I say again, for the villanous treatment (hech!) I have received at your hands in this most untoward (hech!) and unfortunate transaction between us; for (hech!) unfortunate, in every sense, is he that has any-thing to do with (hech!) such a prime and finished impostor."

"You're very warm, Nicky," says Bill; "what puts you into a passion, you old sinner? Sure if it's your own will and pleasure to take exercise at my anvil, *I'm* not to be abused for it. Upon my credit, Nicky, you ought to blush for using such blackguard language, so unbecoming your grave character. You cannot say that it was I set you a hammering at the empty anvil, you profligate. However, as you are so industrious, I simply say it would be a thousand pities to take you from it. Nick, I love industry in my heart, and I always encourage it; so work away, it's not often you spend your time so creditably. I'm afraid if you weren't at that you'd be worse employed."

"Bill, have bowels," said the operative; "you wouldn't go to lay more weight on a falling man, you know; you wouldn't disgrace your character by such a piece of iniquity as keeping an inoffensive gentleman, advanced in years, at such an unbecoming and rascally job as this. Generosity's your top virtue, Bill; not but that you have many other excellent ones, as well as that, among which, as you say yourself, I reckon industry; but still it is in generosity you *shine*. Come, Bill, honour bright, and release me."

"Name the terms, you profligate."

"You're above terms, William; a generous fellow like you never thinks of terms."

"Good bye, old gentleman!" said Bill, very coolly; "I'll drop in to see you once a month."

"No, no, Bill, you infern—a—a—you excellent, worthy, delightful fellow, not so fast; not so fast. Come, name your terms, you sland—my dear Bill, name your terms."

"Seven years more."

"I agree; but—"

"And the same supply of cash as before, down on the nail here."

"Very good; very good. You're rather simple, Bill; rather soft, I must confess. Well, no matter. I shall yet turn the tab— a—hem! You are an exceedingly simple fellow, Bill; still there will come a day, my *dear* Bill—there will come—"

"Do you grumble, you vagrant? Another word, and I double the terms."

"Mum, William—mum; *tace* is Latin for a candle."

"Seven years more of grace, and the same measure of the needful that I got before. Ay or no?"

"Of grace, Bill! Ay! ay! ay! There's the cash. I accept the terms. Oh blood! the rascal—of grace!! Bill!"

"Well, now drop the hammer, and vanish," says Billy; "but what would you think to take this sledge, while you stay, and give me a—eh! why in such a hurry?" he added, seeing that Satan withdrew in double quick time.

"Hollo! Nicholas!" he shouted, "come back; you forgot something!" and when the old gentleman looked behind him, Billy shook the hammer at him, on which he vanished altogether.

Billy now got into his old courses; and what shows the kind of people the world is made of, he also took up with his old company. When they saw that he had the money once more, and was sowing it about him in all directions, they immediately began to find excuses for his former extravagance.

"Say what you will," said one, "Bill Dawson's a spirited fellow, and bleeds like a prince."

"He's a hospitable man in his own house, or out of it, as ever lived," said another.

"His only fault is," observed a third, "that he is, if anything, too generous, and doesn't know the value of money; his fault's on the right side, however."

"He has the spunk in him," said a fourth; "keeps a capital table, prime wines, and a standing welcome for his friends."

"Why," said a fifth, "if he doesn't enjoy his money while he lives, he won't when he's dead; so more power to him, and a wider throat to his purse."

Indeed, the very persons who were cramming themselves at his expense despised him at heart. They knew very well, however, how to take him on the weak side. Praise his generosity, and he would do anything; call him a man of spirit, and you might fleece him to his face. Sometimes he would toss a purse of guineas to this knave, another to that flatterer, a third to a bully, and a fourth to some broken down rake—and all to convince them that *he* was a sterling friend—a man of mettle and liberality. But never was he known to help a virtuous and struggling family—to assist the widow or the fatherless, or to do any other act that was *truly* useful. It is to be supposed the reason of this was, that as he spent it, as most of the world do, in the service of the devil, by whose aid he got it, he was prevented from turning it to a good account. Between you and me, dear reader, there are more persons acting after Bill's fashion in the same world than you dream about.

When his money was out again, his friends played him the same rascally game once more. No sooner did his poverty become plain, than the knaves began to be troubled with small fits of modesty, such as an unwillingness to come to his place when there was no longer any thing to be got there. A kind of virgin bashfulness prevented them from speaking to him when they saw him getting out on the wrong side of his clothes. Many of them would turn away from him in the prettiest and most delicate manner when they thought he wanted to borrow money from them—all for fear of putting him to the blush by asking it. Others again, when they saw him coming towards their houses about dinner hour, would become so confused, from mere gratitude, as to think themselves in another place; and their servants, seized as it were, with the same feeling, would tell Bill that their masters were "not at home."

At length, after travelling the same villanous round as before, Bill was compelled to betake himself, as the last remedy, to the forge; in other words, he found that there is, after all, nothing in this world that a man can rely on so firmly and surely as his own industry.

Bill, however, wanted the organ of common sense; for his experience—and it was sharp enough to leave an impression—ran off him like water off a duck.

He took to his employment sorely against his grain; but he had now no choice. He must either work or starve, and starvation is like a great doctor, nobody tries it till every other remedy fails them. Bill had been twice rich; twice a gentleman among blackguards, but always a blackguard among gentlemen; for no wealth or acquaintance with decent society could rub the rust of his native vulgarity off him. He was now a common blinking sot in his forge; a drunken bully in the tap-room, cursing and brow-beating every one as well as his wife; boasting of how much money he had spent in his day; swaggering about the high doings he carried on; telling stories about himself and Lord This at the Curragh: the dinners he gave—how much they cost him, and attempting to extort credit upon the strength of his former wealth. He was too ignorant, however, to know that he was publishing his own disgrace, and that it was a mean-spirited thing to be proud of what ought to make him blush through a deal board nine inches thick.

He was one morning industriously engaged in a quarrel with his wife, who, with a three-legged stool in her hand, appeared to mistake his head for his

own anvil; he, in the meantime, paid his addresses
to her with his leather apron, when who steps in to
jog his memory about the little agreement that was
between them, but old Nick. The wife, it seems, in
spite of all her exertions to the contrary, was get-
ting the worst of it; and Sir Nicholas, willing to
appear a gentleman of great gallantry, thought he
could not do less than take up the lady's quarrel,
particularly as Bill had laid her in a sleeping pos-
ture. Now Satan thought this too bad; and as he
felt himself under many obligations to the sex, he
determined to defend one of them on the present
occasion; so as Judy rose, he turned upon the hus-
band, and floored him by a clever facer.

"You unmanly villain," said he, "is this the way
you treat your wife? 'Pon honour, Bill, I'll chastise
you on the spot. I could not stand by, a spectator of
such ungentlemanly conduct without giving up all
claim to gallant—" Whack! the word was divided in
his mouth by the blow of a churn-staff from Judy,
who no sooner saw Bill struck, than she nailed
Satan, who "fell" once more.

"What, you villain! that's for striking my hus-
band like a murderer behind his back," said Judy,
and she suited the action to the word, "that's for
interfering between man and wife. Would you mur-
der the poor man before my face? eh? If *he* bates
me, you shabby dog you, who has a better right?
I'm sure it's nothing out of your pocket. Must you
have your finger in every pie?"

This was anything but *idle* talk; for at every word she gave him a remembrance, hot and heavy. Nicholas backed, danced, and hopped; she advanced, still drubbing him with great perseverance, till at length he fell into the redoubtable arm chair, which stood exactly behind him. Bill, who had been putting in two blows for Judy's one, seeing that his enemy was safe, now got between the devil and his wife, *a situation that few will be disposed to envy him.*

"Tenderness, Judy," said the husband, "I hate cruelty. Go put the tongs in the fire, and make them red hot. Nicholas, you have a nose," said he.

Satan began to rise, but was rather surprised to find that he could not budge.

"Nicholas," says Bill, "how is your pulse? you don't look well; that is to say, you look worse than usual."

The other attempted to rise, but found it a mistake.

"I'll thank you to come along," said Bill, "I have a fancy to travel under your guidance, and we'll take the *Low Countries* in our way, won't we? Get to your legs, you sinner; you know a bargain's a bargain between two *honest men,* Nicholas; meaning *yourself* and *me.* Judy, are the tongs hot?"

Satan's face was worth looking at, as he turned his eyes from the husband to the wife, and then fastened them on the tongs, now nearly at a furnace heat in the fire, conscious at the same time that he could not move out of the chair.

"Billy," said he, "you won't forget that I rewarded your generosity the last time I saw you, in the way of business."—"Faith, Nicholas, it fails me to remember any generosity I ever showed you. Don't be womanish. I simply want to see what kind of stuff your nose is made of, and whether it will stretch like a rogue's conscience. If it does, we will flatter it up the *chimly* with the red hot tongs, and when this old hat is fixed on the top of it, let us alone for a weather-cock." —"Have a *fellow-feeling*, Mr. Dawson; you know *we* ought not to dispute. Drop the matter, and I give you the next seven years."—"We know all that," says Billy, opening the red hot tongs very coolly."—"Mr. Dawson," said Satan, "if you cannot remember my friendship to yourself, don't forget how often I stood your father's friend, your grandfather's friend, and the friend of all your relations up to the tenth generation. I intended, also, to stand by your children after you, so long as the name of Dawson, and a respectable one it is, might last."—"Don't be blushing, Nick," says Bill, "you are too modest; that was ever your failing; hould up your head, there's money bid for you. I'll give you such a nose, my good friend, that you will have to keep an outrider before you, to carry the end of it on his shoulder."—"Mr. Dawson, I pledge my honour to raise your children in the world as high as they can go; no matter whether they desire it or not."—"That's very kind of you," says the other, "and I'll do as much for your nose."

He gripped it as he spoke, and the old boy immediately sung out; Bill pulled, and the nose went with him like a piece of warm wax. He then transferred the tongs to Judy, got a ladder, resumed the tongs, ascended the chimney, and tugged stoutly at the nose until he got it five feet above the roof.—He then fixed the hat upon the top of it; and came down.

"There's a weather-cock," said Billy; "I defy Ireland to show such a beauty. Faith, Nick, it would make the purtiest steeple for a church, in all Europe, and the old hat fits it to a shaving."

In this state, with his nose twisted up the chimney, Satan sat for some time, experiencing the novelty of what might be termed a peculiar sensation. At last the worthy husband and wife began to relent:

"I think," said Bill, "that we have made the most of the nose, as well as the joke; I believe, Judy, it's long enough."—"What is?" says Judy.

"Why, the joke," said the husband.

"Faith, and I think so is the nose," said Judy.

"What do you say yourself, Satan?" said Bill.

"Nothing at all, William," said the other; "but that—ha! ha!—it's a good joke—an excellent joke, and a goodly nose, too, as it *stands*. You were always a gentlemanly man, Bill, and did things with a grace; still, if I might give an opinion on such a trifle—"

"It's no trifle at all," says Bill, "if you spake of the nose."—"Very well, it is not," says the other;

"still, both the joke and the nose without further violence, you would lay me under very heavy obligations, which I shall be ready to acknowledge and *repay* as I ought."—"Come," said Bill, "shell out once more, and be off for seven years. As much as you came down with the last time, and vanish."

The words were scarcely spoken, when the money was at his feet, and Satan invisible. Nothing could surpass the mirth of Bill and his wife at the result of this adventure. They laughed till they fell down on the floor.

It is useless to go over the same ground again. Bill was still incorrigible. The money went as the devil's money always goes. Bill caroused and squandered, but could never turn a penny of it to a good purpose. In this way, year after year went, till the seventh was closed, and Bill's hour come. He was now, and had been for some time past, as miserable a knave as ever. Not a shilling had he, nor a shilling's worth, with the exception of his forge, his cabin, and a few articles of crazy furniture. In this state he was standing in his forge as before, straining his ingenuity how to make out a breakfast, when Satan came to look after him. The old gentleman was sorely puzzled how to get at him. He kept skulking and sneaking about the forge for some time, till he saw that Bill hadn't a cross to bless himself with. He immediately changed himself into a guinea, and lay in an open place where he knew Bill would see him. "If," said he, "I get once into his possession, I can manage him." The honest smith took the bait, for it was well gilded, he clutched the guinea, put it into his purse, and closed it up. "Ho! ho!" shouted the devil out of the purse, "you're caught, Bill; I've secured you at last, you knave you. Why don't you despair, you villain, when you think of what's before you."—"Why, you unlucky ould dog," said Bill; "is it there you are? will you always drive your head into every loop-hole that's set for you? Faith, Nick achora, I never had you bagged till now."

Satan then began to tug and struggle with a view of getting out of the purse, but in vain.

"Mr. Dawson," said he, we understand each other. I'll give the seven years additional, and the cash on the nail." "Be aisey, Nicholas. You know the weight of the hammer, that's enough. It's not a whipping with feathers you're going to get, anyhow. Just be aisey." "Mr. Dawson, I grant I'm not your match. Release me, and I double the cash. I was merely trying your temper when I took the shape of a guinea."

"Faith and I'll try yours before you lave it, I've a notion." He immediately commenced with the sledge, and Satan sang out with a considerable want of firmness. "Am I heavy enough!" said Bill.

"Lighter, lighter, William, if you love me. I haven't been well latterly, Mr. Dawson—I have been delicate—my health, in short, is in a very precarious state, Mr. Dawson." "I can believe *that*," said

Bill, "and it will be more so before I have done with you. Am I doing it right?" "Bill," said Nick, is this gentlemanly treatment in your own respectable shop? Do you think, if you dropped into my little place, that I'd act this rascally part towards you? Have you no compunction?" "I know," replied Bill, sledging away with vehemence, "that you're notorious for giving your friends a *warm* welcome. Divil an ould youth more so; but you must be daling in bad coin, must you? However, good or bad, you're in for a sweat now, you sinner. Am I doin' it purty?"

"Lovely, William—but, if possible, a little more delicate."—"Oh, how delicate you are! Maybe a cup o' tay would sarve you, or a little small gruel to compose your stomach."

"Mr. Dawson," said the gentleman in the purse, "hold your hand and let us understand one another. I have a proposal to make."—"Hear the sinner anyhow," said the wife.—"Name your own sum," said Satan, "only set me free."—"No, the sorra may take the toe you'll budge till you let Bill off," said the wife; "hould him hard, Bill, barrin' he sets *you* clear of your engagement."—"There it is, my posy," said Bill; "that's the condition. If you don't give *me up,* here's at you once more—and you must double the cash you gave the last time, too. So, if you're of that opinion, say *ay*—leave the cash and be off."

The money again appeared in a glittering heap before Bill, upon which he exclaimed—"The *ay* has it, you dog. Take to pour pumps now, and fair weather after you, you vagrant; but Nicholas—Nick—here, here—"The other looked back, and saw Bill, with a broad grin upon him, shaking the purse at him—"Nicholas come back," said he, "I'm short a guinea." Nick shook *his* fist, and disappeared.

It would be useless to stop now, merely to inform our readers that Bill was beyond improvement. In short he once more took to his old habits, and lived on exactly in the same manner as before. He had two sons—one as great a blackguard as himself, and who was also named after him; the other was a well-conducted, virtuous young man, called James, who left his father, and having relied upon his own industry and honest perseverance in life, arrived afterwards to great wealth, and built the town called Castle Dawson; which is so called from its founder until this day.

Bill, at length, in spite of all his wealth, was obliged, as he himself said, "to travel,"—in other words, he fell asleep one day, and forgot to awaken; or, in still plainer terms, he died.

Now, it is usual, when a man dies, to close the history of his life and adventures at once; but with our hero this cannot be the case. The moment Bill departed, he very naturally bent his steps towards the residence of St. Moroky, as being, in his opinion, likely to lead him towards the snuggest berth he could readily make out. On arriving he gave a very humble kind of a knock, and St. Moroky appeared.

"God save your Reverence!" said Bill, very submissively.

"Be off: there's no admittance here for so poor a youth as you are," said St. Moroky.

He was now so cold and fatigued that he cared little where he went, provided only, as he said himself, "he could rest his bones, and get an air of the fire." Accordingly, after arriving at a large black gate, he knocked, as before, and was told he would get *instant* admittance the moment he gave his name.

"Billy Dawson," he replied.

"Off, instantly," said the porter to his companions, "and let his Majesty know that the rascal he dreads so much is here at the gate."

Such a racket and tumult were never heard as the very mention of Billy Dawson created.

In the meantime, his old acquaintance came running towards the gate with such haste and consternation, that his tail was several times nearly tripping up his heels.

"Don't admit that rascal," he shouted; "bar the gate—make every chain, and lock, and bolt, fast—I won't be safe—and I won't stay here, nor none of us need stay here, if he gets in—my bones are sore yet after him. No, no—begone you villain—you'll get no entrance here—I know you too well."

Bill could not help giving a broad, malicious grin at Satan, and, putting his nose through the bars, he exclaimed—"Ha! you ould dog, I have you afraid of me at last, have I?"

He had scarcely uttered the words, when his foe, who stood inside, instantly tweaked him by the nose, and Bill felt as if he had been gripped by the same red-hot tongs with which he himself had formerly tweaked the nose of Nicholas.

Bill then departed, but soon found that in consequence of the inflammable materials which strong drink had thrown into his nose, that organ immediately took fire, and, indeed, to tell the truth, kept burning night and day, winter and summer, without ever once going out, from that hour to this.

Such was the sad fate of Billy Dawson, who has been walking without stop or stay, from place to place ever since; and in consequence of the flame on his nose, and his beard being tangled like a wisp of hay, he has been christened by the country folk Will-o'-the-Wisp, while as it were, to show the mischief of his disposition, the circulating knave, knowing that he must seek the coldest bogs and quagmires in order to cool his nose, seizes upon that opportunity of misleading the unthinking and tipsy night travellers from their way, just that he may have the satisfaction of still taking in as many as possible.

A Legend of Knockmany

WILLIAM CARLETON

What Irish man, woman, or child, has not heard of our renowned Hibernian Hercules, the great and glorious Fin M'Coul? Not one, from Cape Clear to the Giant's Causeway, nor from that back again to Cape Clear. And by the way, speaking of the Giant's Causeway brings me at once to the beginning of my story. Well, it so happened that Fin and his gigantic relatives were all working at the Causeway, in order to make a bridge, or what was still better, a good stout padroad, across to Scotland; when Fin, who was very fond of his wife Oonagh, took it into his head that he would go home and see how the poor woman got on in his absence. To be sure, Fin was a true Irishman, and so the sorrow thing in life brought him back, only to see that she was snug and comfortable, and, above all things, that she got her rest well at night; for he knew that the poor woman, when he was with her, used to be subject to nightly qualms and configurations, that kept him a very anxious, decent man, striving to keep her up to the good spirits and health that she had when they were first married. So, accordingly, he pulled up a fir-tree, and, after lopping off the roots and branches, made a walking-stick of it, and set out on his way to Oonagh.

Oonagh, or rather Fin, lived at this time on the very tip-top of Knockmany Hill, which faces a cousin of its own, called Cullamore, that rises up, half-hill, half-mountain, on the opposite side— east-east by south, as the sailors say, when they wish to puzzle a landsman.

Now, the truth is, for it must come out, that honest Fin's affection for his wife, though cordial enough in itself, was by no manner or means the real cause of his journey home. There was at that time another giant, named Cucullin—some say he was Irish, and some say he was Scotch—but whether Scotch or Irish, sorrow doubt of it but he was a *targer*. No other giant of the day could stand before him; and such was his strength, that, when well vexed, he could give a stamp that shook the country about him. The fame and name of him went far and near; and nothing in the shape of a man, it was said, had any chance with him in a fight. Whether the story is true or not, I cannot say, but the report went that, by one blow of his fist, he flattened a thunderbolt, and kept it in his pocket, in the shape of a pancake, to show to all his enemies when they were about to fight him. Undoubtedly

he had given every giant in Ireland a considerable
beating, barring Fin M'Coul himself; and he swore,
by the solemn contents of Moll Kelly's Primer, that
he would never rest, night or day, winter or sum-
mer, till he would serve Fin with the same sauce,
if he could catch him. Fin, however, who no doubt
was the cock of the walk on his own dunghill, had
a strong disinclination to meet a giant who could
make a young earthquake, or flatten a thunderbolt
when he was angry; so he accordingly kept dodg-
ing about from place to place, not much to his
credit as a Trojan, to be sure, whenever he hap-
pened to get the hard word that Cucullin was on
the scent of him. This, then, was the marrow of the
whole movement, although he put it on his anxi-
ety to see Oonagh; and I am not saying but there
was some truth in that too. However, the short and
the long of it was, with reverence be it spoken, that
he heard Cucullin was coming to the Causeway to
have a trial of strength with him; and he was natu-
rally enough seized, in consequence, with a very
warm and sudden fit of affection for his wife, poor
woman, who was delicate in her health, and lead-
ing, besides, a very lonely uncomfortable life of it
(he assured them), in his absence. He accordingly
pulled up the fir-tree, as I said before, and having
snedded it into a walking-stick, set out on his affec-
tionate travels to see his darling Oonagh on the
top of Knockmany, by the way.

In truth, to state the suspicions of the country at the time, the people wondered very much why it was that Fin selected such a windy spot for his dwelling-house, and they even went so far as to tell him as much.

"What can you mane, Mr. M'Coul," said they, "by pitching your tent upon the top of Knockmany, where you never are without a breeze, day or night, winter or summer, and where you're often forced to take your nightcap without either going to bed or turning up your little finger; ay, an' where, besides this, there's the sorrow's own want of water?"

"Why," said Fin, "ever since I was the height of a round tower, I was known to be fond of having a good prospect of my own; and where the dickens, neighbours, could I find a better spot for a good prospect than the top of Knockmany? As for water, I am sinking a pump, and, plase goodness, as soon as the Causeway's made, I intend to finish it."

Now, this was more of Fin's philosophy; for the real state of the case was, that he pitched upon the top of Knockmany in order that he might be able to see Cucullin coming towards the house, and, of course, that he himself might go to look after his distant transactions in other parts of the country, rather than—but no matter—wc do not wish to be too hard on Fin. All we have to say is, that if he wanted a spot from which to keep a sharp look-out—and, between ourselves, he did want it grievously—barring Slieve Croob, or Slieve Donard, or its own cousin, Cullamore, he could not find a neater or more convenient situation for it in the sweet and sagacious province of Ulster.

"God save all here!" said Fin, good humouredly, on putting his honest face into his own door.

"Musha Fin, avick, an' you're welcome home to your own Oonagh, you darlin' bully." Here followed a smack that is said to have made the waters of the lake at the bottom of the hill curl, as it were, with kindness and sympathy.

"Faith," said Fin, "beautiful; an' how are you, Oonagh—and how did you sport your figure during my absence, my bilberry?"

"Never a merrier—as bouncing a grass widow as ever there was in sweet 'Tyrone among the bushes.'"

Fin gave a short good-humoured cough, and laughed most heartily, to show her how much he was delighted that she made herself happy in his absence.

"An' what brought you home so soon, Fin?" said she.

"Why, avourneen," said Fin, putting in his answer in the proper way, "never the thing but the purest of love and affection for yourself. Sure you know that's truth, any how, Oonagh."

Fin spent two or three happy days with Oonagh, and felt himself very comfortable, considering the dread he had of Cucullin. This, however, grew upon him so much that his wife could not but perceive that something lay on his mind which he kept altogether to himself. Let a woman alone, in the meantime, for ferreting or wheedling a secret out of her good man, when she wishes. Fin was a proof of this.

"It's this Cucullin," said Fin, "that's troubling me. When the fellow gets angry, and begins to stamp, he'll shake you a whole townland; and it's well known that he can stop a thunderbolt, for he always carries one about him in the shape of a pancake, to show to any one that might misdoubt it."

As he spoke, he clapped his thumb in his mouth, which he always did when he wanted to prophesy, or to know any thing that happened in his absence; and the wife, who knew what he did it for, said, very sweetly,

"Fin, darling, I hope you don't bite your thumb at me, dear?"

"No," said Fin; "but I bite my thumb, acushla," said he.

"Yes, jewel; but, take care and don't draw blood," said she. "Ah, Fin! don't, my bully—don't."

"He's coming," said Fin; "I see him below Dungannon."

"Thank goodness, dear! an' who is it, avick? Glory be to God!"

"That baste Cucullin," replied Fin; "and how to manage I don't know. If I run away, I am disgraced; and I know that sooner or later I must meet him, for my thumb tells me so."

"When will he be here?" said she.

"To-morrow, about two o'clock," replied Fin, with a groan.

"Well, my bully, don't be cast down," said Oonagh; "depend on me, and maybe I'll bring you better out of this scrape than ever you could bring yourself, by your rule o' thumb."

This quieted Fin's heart very much, for he knew that Oonagh was hand and glove with the fairies; and, indeed, to tell the truth, she was supposed to be a fairy herself. If she was, however, she must have been a kind-hearted one; for, by all accounts, she never did any thing but good in the neighbourhood.

Now, it so happened that Oonagh had a sister named Granua, living opposite them, on the very top of Cullamore, which I have mentioned already, and this Granua was quite as powerful as herself. The beautiful valley that lies between them is not more than about three or four miles broad, so that of a summer's evening, Granua and Oonagh were able to hold many an agreeable conversation across it, from the one hill-top to the other. Upon this occasion, Oonagh resolved to consult her sister as to what was best to be done in the difficulty that surrounded them.

"Granua," said she, "are you at home?"

"No," said the other; "I'm picking bilberries in Althadhawan" (*Anglicé*, the Devil's Glen).

"Well," said Oonagh, "get up to the top of Cullamore, look about you, and then tell us what you see."

"Very well," replied Granua, after a few minutes, "I am there now."

"What do you see?" asked the other.

"Goodness be about us!" exclaimed Granua, "I see the biggest giant that ever was known, coming up from Dungannon."

"Ay," said Oonagh, "there's our difficulty. That giant is the great Cucullin; and he's now comin' up to leather Fin. What's to be done?"

"I'll call to him," she replied, "to come up to Cullamore, and refresh himself, and maybe that will give you and Fin time to think of some plan to get yourselves out of the scrape. "But," she proceeded, "I'm short of butter, having in the house only half a dozen firkins, and as I'm to have a few giants and giantesses to spend the evenin' with me, I'd feel thankful, Oonagh, if you'd throw me up fifteen or sixteen tubs, or the largest miscaun you have got, and you'll oblige me very much."

"I'll do that with a heart and a half," replied Oonagh; "and, indeed, Granua, I feel myself under great obligations to you for your kindness in keeping him off of us, till we see what can be done; for what would become of us all if any thing happened Fin, poor man?"

She accordingly got the largest miscaun of butter she had—which might be about the weight of a couple dozen millstones, so that you may easily judge of its size—and calling up to her sister, "Granua," said she, "are you ready? I'm going to throw you up a miscaun, so be prepared to catch it."

"I will," said the other; "a good throw now, and take care it does not fall short."

Oonagh threw it; but in consequence of her anxiety about Fin and Cucullin, she forgot to say the charm that was to send it up, so that, instead of reaching Cullamore, as she expected, it fell about half way between the two hills, at the edge of the Broad Bog near Augher.

"My curse upon you!" she exclaimed; "you've disgraced me. I now change you into a grey stone. Lie there as a testimony of what has happened; and may evil betide the first living man that will ever attempt to remove or injure you!"

And, sure enough, there it lies to this day, with the mark of the four fingers and thumb imprinted in it, exactly as it came out of her hand.

"Never mind," said Granua; "I must only do the best I can with Cucullin. If all fad, I'll give him a cast of heather broth to keep the wind out of his stomach, or a panada of oakbark to draw it in a bit; but, above all things, think of some plan to get Fin out of the scrape he's in, otherwise he's a lost man. You know you used to be sharp and ready-witted; and my own opinion, Oonagh, is, that it will go hard with you, or you'll outdo Cucullin yet."

She then made a high smoke on the top of the hill, after which she put her finger in her mouth, and gave three whistles, and by that Cucullin knew he was invited to Cullamore—for this was the way that the Irish long ago gave a sign to all strangers and travellers, to let them know they were welcome to come and take share of whatever was going.

In the meantime, Fin was very melancholy, and did not know what to do, or how to act at all. Cucullin was an ugly customer, no doubt, to meet with; and, moreover, the idea of the confounded "cake" aforesaid, flattened the very heart within him. What chance could he have, strong and brave though he was, with a man who could, when put into a passion, walk the country into earthquakes and knock thunderbolts into pancakes? The thing was impossible; and Fin knew not on what hand to turn him. Right or left—backward or forward— where to go he could form no guess whatsoever.

"Oonagh," said he, "can you do nothing for me? Where's all your invention? Am I to be skivered like a rabbit before your eyes, and to have my name disgraced for ever in the sight of all my tribe, and me the best man among them? How am I to fight this man-mountain—this huge cross between an earthquake and a thunderbolt?—with a pancake in his pocket that was once—"

"Be easy, Fin," replied Oonagh; "troth, I'm ashamed of you. Keep your toe in your pump, will you? Talking of pancakes, maybe we'll give him as good as any he brings with him—thunderbolt or otherwise. If I don't treat him to as smart feeding as he's got this many a day, never trust Oonagh again. Leave him to me, and do just as I bid you."

This relieved Fin very much; for, after all, he had great confidence in his wife, knowing, as he did, that she had got him out of many a quandary before. The present, however, was the greatest of all; but still he began to get courage, and was able to eat his victuals as usual. Oonagh then drew the nine woollen threads of different colours, which she always did to find out the best way of succeeding in any thing of importance she went about. She then platted them into three plats with three colours in each, putting one on her right arm, one round her heart, and the third round her right ankle, for then she knew that nothing could fail with her that she undertook.

Having every thing now prepared, she sent round to the neighbours and borrowed one-and-twenty iron griddles, which she took and kneaded into the hearts of one-and-twenty cakes of bread, and these she baked on the fire in the usual way, setting them aside in the cupboard according as they were done. She then put down a large pot of new milk, which she made into curds and whey, and gave Fin due instructions how to use the curds when Cucullin should come. Having done all this, she sat down quite contented, waiting for his arrival on the next day about two o'clock, that being the hour at which he was expected—for Fin knew as much by the sucking of his thumb. Now, this was a curious property that Fin's thumb had; but, notwithstanding all the wisdom and logic he used to suck out of it, it could never have stood to him here were it not for the wit of his wife. In this very thing, moreover, he was very much resembled by his great foe Cucullin; for it was well known that the huge strength he possessed all lay in the middle finger of his right hand, and that, if he happened by any mischance to lose it, he was no more, notwithstanding his bulk, than a common man.

At length, the next day, he was seen coming across the valley, and Oonagh knew that it was time to commence operations. She immediately made the cradle, and desired Fin to lie down in it, and cover himself up with the clothes.

"You must pass for your own child," said she; "so just lie there snug, and say nothing, but be guided by me." This, to be sure, was wormwood to Fin—I mean going into the cradle in such a cowardly manner—but he knew Oonagh well; and finding that he had nothing else for it, with a very rueful face he gathered himself into it, and lay snug as she had desired him.

About two o'clock, as he had been expected, Cucullin came in. "God save all here!" said he; "is this where the great Fin M'Coul lives?"

"Indeed it is, honest man," replied Oonagh; "God save you kindly—won't you be sitting?"

"Thank you, ma'am," says he, sitting down; "you're Mrs. M'Coul, I suppose?"

"I am," said she; "and I have no reason, I hope, to be ashamed of my husband."

"No," said the other; "he has the name of being the strongest and bravest man in Ireland; but for all that, there's a man not far from you that's very desirous of taking a shake with him. Is he at home?"

"Why, then, no," she replied; "and if ever a man left his house in a fury, he did. It appears that some one told him of a big basthoon of a giant called Cucullin being down at the Causeway to look for him, and so he set out there to try if he could catch him. Troth, I hope, for the poor giant's sake, he won't meet with him, for if he does, Fin will make paste of him at once."

"Well," said the other, "I am Cucullin, and I have been seeking him these twelvemonths, but he always kept clear of me; and I will never rest night or day till I lay my hands on him."

At this Oonagh set up a loud laugh, of great contempt, by the way, and looked at him as if he was only a mere handful of a man.

"Did you ever see Fin?" said she, changing her manner all at once.

"How could I?" said he; "he always took care to keep his distance."

"I thought so," she replied; "I judged as much; and if you take my advice, you poor-looking creature, you'll pray night and day that you may never see him, for I tell you it will be a black day for you when you do. But, in the mean time, you perceive that the wind's on the door, and as Fin himself is from home, maybe you'd be civil enough to turn the house, for it's always what Fin does when he's here."

This was a startler even to Cucullin; but he got up, however, and after pulling the middle finger of his right hand until it cracked three times, he went outside, and getting his arms about the house, completely turned it as she had wished. When Fin saw this, he felt a certain description of moisture, which shall be nameless, oozing out through every pore of his skin; but Oonagh, depending upon her woman's wit, felt not a whit daunted.

"Arrah, then," said she, "as you are so civil, maybe you'd do another obliging turn for us, as Fin's not here to do it himself. You see, after this long stretch of dry weather we've had, we feel very badly off for want of water. Now, Fin says there's a fine spring-well somewhere under the rocks behind the hill here below, and it was his intention to pull them asunder; but having heard of you, he left the place in such a fury, that he never thought of it. Now, if you try to find it, troth I'd feel it a kindness."

She then brought Cucullin down to see the place, which was then all one solid rock; and, after looking at it for some time, he cracked his right middle finger nine times, and, stooping down, tore a cleft about four hundred feet deep, and a quarter of a mile in length, which has since been christened by the name of Lumford's Glen. This feat nearly threw Oonagh herself off her guard; but what won't a woman's sagacity and presence of mind accomplish?

"You'll now come in," said she, "and eat a bit of such humble fare as we can give you. Fin, even although he and you are enemies, would scorn not to treat you kindly in his own house; and, indeed, if I didn't do it even in his absence, he would not be pleased with me."

She accordingly brought him in, and placing half a dozen of the cakes we spoke of before him, together with a can or two of butter, a side of boiled bacon, and a stack of cabbage, she desired him to help himself—for this, be it known, was long before the invention of potatoes. Cucullin, who, by the way, was a glutton as well as a hero, put one of the cakes in his mouth to take a huge whack out of it, when both Fin and Oonagh were stunned with a noise that resembled something between a growl and a yell. "Blood and fury!" he shouted; "how is this? Here are two of my teeth out! What kind of bread is this you gave me?"

"What's the matter?" said Oonagh coolly.

"Matter!" shouted the other again; "why, here are the two best teeth in my head gone!"

"Why," said she, "that's Fin's bread—the only bread he ever eats when at home; but, indeed, I forgot to tell you that nobody can eat it but himself, and that child in the cradle there. I thought, however, that, as you were reported to be rather a stout little fellow of your size, you might be able to manage it, and I did not wish to affront a man that thinks himself able to fight Fin. Here's another cake—maybe it's not so hard as that."

Cucullin at the moment was not only hungry but ravenous, so he accordingly made a fresh set at the second cake, and immediately another yell was heard twice as loud as the first. "Thunder and giblets!" he roared, "take your bread out of this, or I will not have a tooth in my head; there's another pair of them gone!"

"Well, honest man," replied Oonagh, "if you're not able to eat the bread, say so quietly, and don't be wakening the child in the cradle there. There, now, he's awake upon me."

Fin now gave a skirl that startled the giant, as coming from such a youngster as he was represented to be. "Mother," said he, "I'm hungry—get me something to eat." Oonagh went over, and putting into his hand a cake *that had no griddle in it*, Fin, whose appetite in the meantime was sharpened by what he saw going forward, soon made it disappear. Cucullin was thunderstruck, and secretly thanked his stars that he had the good fortune to miss meeting Fin, for, as he said to himself, I'd have no chance with a man who could eat such bread as that, which even his son that's but in his cradle can munch before my eyes.

"I'd like to take a glimpse at the lad in the cradle," said he to Oonagh; "for I can tell you that the infant who can manage that nutriment is no joke to look at, or to feed of a scarce summer."

"With all the veins of my heart," replied Oonagh. "Get up, acushla, and show this decent little man something that won't be unworthy of your father, Fin M'Coul."

Fin, who was dressed for the occasion as much like a boy as possible, got up, and bringing Cucullin out—"Are you strong?" said he.

"Thunder an' ounds!" exclaimed the other, "what a voice in so small a chap!"

"Are you strong?" said Fin again; "are you able to squeeze water out of that white stone?" he asked, putting one into Cucullin's hand. The latter squeezed and squeezed the stone, but to no purpose: he might pull the rocks of Lumford's Glen asunder, and flatten a thunderbolt, but to squeeze water out of a white stone was beyond his strength. Fin eyed him with great contempt, as he kept straining and squeezing, and squeezing and straining, till he got black in the face with the efforts.

"Ah, you're a poor creature!" said Fin. "You a giant! Give me the stone here, and when I'll show what Fin's little son can do, you may then judge of what my daddy himself is."

Fin then took the stone, and slily exchanging it for the curds, he squeezed the latter until the whey, as clear as water, oozed out in a little shower from his hand.

"I'll now go in," said he, "to my cradle; for I'd scorn to lose my time with any one that's not able to eat my daddy's bread, or squeeze water out of a stone. Bedad, you had better be off out of this before he comes back; for if he catches you, it's in flummery he'd have you in two minutes."

Cucullin, seeing what he had seen, was of the same opinion himself; his knees knocked together with the terror of Fin's return, and he accordingly hastened in to bid Oonagh farewell, and to assure her, that from that day out, he never wished to hear of, much less to see, her husband. "I admit fairly that I'm not a match for him," said he, "strong as I am; tell him I will avoid him as I would the plague, and that I will make myself scarce in this part of the country while I live."

Fin, in the mean time, had gone into the cradle, where he lay very quietly, his heart at his mouth with delight that Cucullin was about to take his departure, without discovering the tricks that had been played off on him.

"It's well for you," said Oonagh, "that he doesn't happen to be here, for it's nothing but hawk's meat he'd make of you."

"I know that," says Cucullin; "divil a thing else he'd make of me; but before I go, will you let me feel what kind of teeth they are that can eat griddle-bread like *that?*"—and he pointed to it as he spoke.

"With all pleasure in life," said she; "only, as they're far back in his head, you must put your finger a good way in."

Cucullin was surprised to find such a powerful set of grinders in one so young; but he was still much more so on finding, when he took his hand from Fin's mouth, that he had left the very finger upon which his whole strength depended, behind him. He gave one loud groan, and fell down at once with terror and weakness. This was all Fin wanted, who now knew that his most powerful and bitterest enemy was completely at his mercy. He instantly started out of the cradle, and in a few minutes the great Cucullin, that was for such a length of time the terror of him and all his followers, lay a corpse before him. Thus did Fin, through the wit and invention of Oonagh, his wife, succeed in overcoming his enemy by stratagem, which he never could have done by force; and thus also is it proved that the women, if they bring us *into* many an unpleasant scrape, can sometimes succeed in getting us *out of* others that are as bad.

The Lepracaun,
or,
Fairy Shoemaker

WILLIAM ALLINGHAM

I

Little Cowboy, what have you heard,
    Up on the lonely rath's green mound?
Only the plaintive yellow bird
    Sighing in sultry fields around,
Chary, chary, chary, chee-ee!—
Only the grasshopper and the bee?—
        "Tip-tap, rip-rap,
        Tick-a-tack-too!
    Scarlet leather, sewn together,
        This will make a shoe.
    Left, right, pull it tight;
        Summer days are warm;
    Underground in winter,
        Laughing at the storm!"

Lay your ear close to the hill.
Do you not catch the tiny clamour,
Busy click of an elfin hammer,
Voice of the Lepracaun singing shrill
    As he merrily plies his trade?
        He's a span
        And a quarter in height.
    Get him in sight, hold him tight,
        And you're a made
           Man!

II

You watch your cattle the summer day,
Sup on potatoes, sleep in the hay;
    How would you like to roll in your carriage,
    Look for a duchess's daughter in marriage?
Seize the Shoemaker—then you may!
        "Big boots a-hunting,
        Sandals in the hall,
    White for a wedding-feast,
        Pink for a ball.
    This way, that way,
        So we make a shoe;
    Getting rich every stitch,
        Tick-tack-too!"

Nine-and-ninety treasure-crocks
This keen miser-fairy hath,
Hid in mountains, woods, and rocks,
Ruin and round-tow'r, cave and rath,
  And where the cormorants build;
    From times of old
    Guarded by him;
    Each of them fill'd
    Full to the brim
      With gold!

III

I caught him at work one day, myself,
  In the castle-ditch where foxglove grows,—
A wrinkled, wizen'd, and bearded Elf,
  Spectacles stuck on his pointed nose,
  Silver buckles to his hose,
  Leather apron—shoe in his lap—
    "Rip-rap, tip-tap,
    Tack-tack-too!
  (A grasshopper on my cap!
    Away the moth flew!)
  Buskins for a fairy prince,
    Brogues for his son,—
  Pay me well, pay me well,
    When the job is done!"

The rogue was mine, beyond a doubt.
I stared at him; he stared at me;
"Servant, Sir!" "Humph!" says he,
    And pull'd a snuff-box out.
He took a long pinch, look'd better pleased,
    The queer little Lepracaun;
Offer'd the box with a whimsical grace,—
Pouf! he flung the dust in my face,
    And, while I sneezed,
        Was gone!

Original Sources

Allingham, William. "The Fairies," *Irish Songs and Poems*. London: Longmans Green and Company, 1901.

———. "The Lepracaun, or, Fairy Shoemaker," *Poems*. London: Chapman and Hall, 1850.

Anonymous. "The Witch of Rathdowney," *The Dublin University Magazine*, October, 1839.

Carleton, William. "The Fate of Frank M'Kenna," *Tales and Sketches Illustrating the Character, Usages, Traditions, Sports and Pastimes of the Irish Peasantry*. London: James Duffy, 1854.

———. "The Three Wishes," *Tuber Durg; or, the Red Well. Party Fight and Funeral, Dandy Keyhoe's Christening, and Other Irish Tales*. London: James Duffy, 1869.

———. "A Legend of Knockmany," *Tales and Sketches Illustrating the Character, Usages, Traditions, Sports and Pastimes of the Irish Peasantry*. London: James Duffy, 1854.

Croker, T. Crofton. "The Bunworth Banshee," *Fairy Legends and Traditions of the South of Ireland.* London: John Murray, 1825.

————. "The Lady of Gollerus," *Fairy Legends and Traditions of the South of Ireland: Part II.* London: John Murray, 1828.

————. "The Priest's Supper," *Fairy Legends and Traditions of the South of Ireland.* London: John Murray, 1825.

Maclintock, Letitia. "Pat Diver's Ordeal," *The Dublin University Magazine,* February, 1877.

E.W. "The Pooka," *The Dublin Penny Journal,* July 4, 1835.

Lady Wilde. "The Changeling," *Ancient Legends, Mystic Charms, and Superstitions of Ireland.* Boston: Ticknor and Company, 1888.

————. "The Priest's Soul," *Ancient Legends, Mystic Charms, and Superstitions of Ireland.* Boston: Ticknor and Company, 1888.